Doing Middle Leade

C000139565

Are you a new or aspiring middle leader? Or have you been doing the job for a while but want some practical tips to ease workload and support your staff? This book draws together real experiences of middle leadership, both good and bad, and offers practical tips to help you find your voice, support your team, act with integrity and work with the Senior Leadership Team to improve your school.

Covering all aspects of middle leadership including leadership styles, pedagogical approaches, the role of social media, how to tackle difficult conversations, staff wellbeing and much more, the authors will help you avoid common pitfalls, navigate highs and lows, and develop a school environment that enables both students and staff to flourish.

For any new, experienced or prospective middle-leader *Doing Middle Leadership Right* provides a professional insight into how to lead with humanity at the centre of your practice. It puts staff and their wellbeing first – focussing not only on how to have the highest standards for both students and staff but also how to lead ethically.

Lyndsay Bawden is a trust-wide English lead and a former HoD, Lead Practitioner and SLE. She works with SLT and English teams to provide CPD, mentoring and coaching, curriculum design and to support with improvement strategies.

Jade Hickin has been a teacher of English for over ten years and is a former Head of Department. She is currently working as a Trust-Wide Lead Practitioner for English as well as the Whole-School Lead Practitioner for Teaching and Learning in a MAT.

Kaley Macis-Riley works as the Head of English, Drama and Whole-School Lead for Literacy at a school in Derbyshire. Alongside her teaching commitments, Kaley runs an education consultancy business, HoDandHeart, offering CPD to teachers and leaders globally.

'*Doing Middle Leadership Right* is an honest and incredibly useful account of the roles and responsibilities of middle leaders. It is excellent that colleagues in these roles have more information and insights than they had in the past. And this book by Lyndsay Bawden, Jade Hickin and Kaley Macis-Riley is carefully evidenced and brilliantly brought to life with compelling case studies. DMLR is going to make a real difference to the knowledge and confidence of middle leader colleagues. Highly recommended.'

Mary Myatt, Education adviser and writer

'Middle leadership is a dizzying rollercoaster ride and this book reflects that. It takes you on a whistle-stop tour of contemporary educational thinking, rich in examples and case studies of those who are doing the job daily, and giving the reader bite-sized insights to take away and think over. For anyone new to a head of department role, this book will be helpful in making sense of the jargon and buzzwords that can bamboozle us and will hopefully help them sort out what really matters in the role from the surrounding clamour to attempt to do it all.

Doing Middle Leadership Right is written with humour and humility. The book may list three authors but their work has been supported by dozens of others who are cited throughout the work and whose ideas come together in these pages.'

Mark Enser, Head of Geography and Research Lead,
author of The CPD Curriculum

'This book enters the world of education literature at exactly the right time as conversations about the need to improve middle leadership training, support and CPD abound. After all, middle leadership is a role that so many aspire to and yet so many find themselves fulfilling without training and, sadly, often without guidance. This book is thus an essential read for all - regardless of experience.

Packed with sage advice, relatable case studies and tangible action points, this is a book that I wish I'd had in those early years when beginning my middle leadership career. The authors have done an incredible job of covering every area of middle leadership; from curriculum development to flexible working, from difficult conversations to teaching and learning theory. It will challenge, reassure and inspire you in equal measure.'

Kate Stockings, Head of Geography

Doing Middle Leadership Right

A Practical Guide to Leading with Honesty and Integrity in Schools

Lyndsay Bawden, Jade Hickin, and Kaley Macis-Riley

Routledge
Taylor & Francis Group

LONDON AND NEW YORK

Cover Art and Illustrations by David Goodwin of Organise Ideas

First published 2022
by Routledge
4 Park Square, Milton Park, Abingdon, Oxon OX14 4RN

and by Routledge
605 Third Avenue, New York, NY 10158

Routledge is an imprint of the Taylor & Francis Group, an informa business

British Library Cataloguing-in-Publication Data
A catalogue record for this book is available from the British Library

Library of Congress Cataloguing-in-Publication Data
Names: Bawden, Lyndsay, author. | Macis-Riley, Kaley, author. | Hickin, Jade, author.
Title: Doing middle leadership right : a practical guide to leading with honesty and integrity in schools / Lyndsay Bawden, Kaley Macis-Riley and Jade Hickin.
Description: Abingdon, Oxon ; New York, NY : Routledge, 2022. | Includes bibliographical references and index.
Identifiers: LCCN 2021052874 | ISBN 9780367749705 (hardback) | ISBN 9780367749699 (paperback) | ISBN 9781003160557 (ebook)
Subjects: LCSH: Educational leadership--Moral and ethical aspects. | School management and organization--Moral and ethical aspects. | Middle managers--In-service training.
Classification: LCC LB2806 .B3568 2022 | DDC 371.2/011--dc23/eng/20220124
LC record available at https://lccn.loc.gov/2021052874

ISBN: 978-0-367-74970-5 (hbk)
ISBN: 978-0-367-74969-9 (pbk)
ISBN: 978-1-003-16055-7 (ebk)

DOI: 10.4324/9781003160557

Typeset in Melior
by MPS Limited, Dehradun

Contents

Foreword

Middle leadership is tough. There is a lot of responsibility and accountability on top of a heavy teaching timetable. Different middle leadership roles bring different challenges. A Head of Department or phase leader will have deadlines and administration to deal with as well as ensuring a breadth and depth of subject knowledge and expertise within their departments and key stage teams. Pastoral leaders also have the deadlines and data, but this role tends to be more reactive and responsive. This can also feel like a constant fast pace of change; from government reforms to examination changes and leading in times of uncertainty. Lyndsay is right; middle leadership can be exhausting. Middle leaders play a vital role in every school community as not only do they lead change, they are heavily and actively involved in implementing that change too.

Despite the challenges and demands of middle leadership, it can be incredibly rewarding and enjoyable. Middle leaders have close relationships with the teams they lead and support, as well as maintaining close working relationships with students in their classes. Middle leaders can get the best of both worlds with a leadership role whilst staying in the classroom, which is absolutely the best place to be in a school. Middle leaders truly can make a difference and have a positive impact. Lyndsay is also right that '*the glue that holds us all together, is the middle leadership*' in a school.

I have held various middle leadership roles in three different schools. Most of my teaching career has been as a middle leader and I haven't always got this right. Jade has summed it up well, that she has worked with inspiring middle leaders and also worked with those who although well-intentioned simply got it so wrong. Middle leadership is too important to get wrong. Doing middle leadership right is essential; for the teachers and students they support and the senior leaders that delegate and trust them to do the best they possibly can.

On reflection, I should have sought more advice, asked more questions, recognised when I needed support and learned from other leaders around me. I wish I had this book earlier in my career to support me in my role as a middle leader to make sure I get it right for myself and those around me. Kaley has stated that she is the leader she is today because of those she has worked with, showing the ripple effect of leaders and how we can forget the influence we have on others. We can learn from all those in leadership, those who show us how it's done well and those who show us how not to do it!

Jade, Kaley and Lyndsay have come together as a middle leadership dream team combining their wealth of knowledge, insight, experiences and expertise. They have also enlisted a wide range of voices to add to the rich discussion about getting middle leadership right from the classroom teacher to CEO. It is inspiring and empowering to read a powerful female collaboration writing about leadership too.

I have wondered, is it possible to be the best teacher I can be as well as a middle leader? Has being a middle leader had a negative impact on my teaching or has my passion for teaching and learning taken my focus away from middle leadership? It is certainly possible, and should be the case, that all middle leaders lead by example in all they do, from communication to well-being and of course their teaching in the classroom day in and day out. This book supports middle leaders' grasp as to how this can be achieved.

In recent years, the teaching profession has become evidence-informed, enthusiastically embracing the findings from research and applying that to the classroom. *Doing Middle Leadership Right* shows how leaders can and should embrace research from curriculum design to lesson observations and much more. I have a well-known passion for learning about cognitive psychology so I was delighted to read about this in a middle leadership book, as it should be. Leaders at all levels play an important role in any school community truly becoming evidence-informed as the authors have illustrated.

I would recommend this book for aspiring, current and experienced middle leaders. The breadth and depth that this book covers is very impressive. It is an informative and interesting read with heart and warmth too as Kaley beautifully writes: *"May we lead with our hearts, always"*.

This is a book middle leaders will read and take so much away from but will also return to again and then recommend to others as we encourage those we lead to become middle leaders too. This book provides advice, guidance, research and experiences to help ensure those who work in schools do middle leadership right.

Kate Jones

Acknowledgements

Lyndsay:

Thank you to my husband for believing in me, and also for looking after me and the kids while I wrote two books and studied for a Master's whilst working full time (who needs free time, right?).

Thanks to my oldest and most wonderful friend Libby Allen for proofreading the book so carefully and helping us with her wise and thoughtful comments, and for putting up with me for the last 30 years.

Finally, thanks to my friends IRL and in my phone – 'The xxxxingdons' and 'PLG2' – you know who you are!

Jade:

For my children, Margot and Rufus: thank you for putting up with Mummy hiding away in the study; you are and always will be the axis of my world.

And for Scout – my favourite.

For my friends: thank you for supporting me through the hardest of times. I literally wouldn't be here without you.

And a special thanks to David Goodwin for his help, support and beautiful images!

Kaley:

For those in my life who have inspired me to lead with heart: my parents, my little brother, the calm in my storm that is my husband and my friends (both those I've met in real life, and the ***tingdons in my phone). Your ongoing support has given me the courage to put my (now double-barrelled) name in print twice! Thank you.

For Scarlett Jayne: may you be led with heart and be confident to challenge it when you're not, and eventually lead with your own in whatever path you take.

Finally, thanks to the leaders I've worked with – good and bad – for moulding me into the leader that I am today. Not forgetting the two (exceptional) leaders with whom I wrote this book: I'm so incredibly grateful to have you both in my life, no matter how frequently I 'flounce'.

From all of us:

All three of us are honoured to have had Kate Jones write such a beautiful foreword, making this a true female powerhouse of a book!

And a final thank you from all three of us to all those who proofread, offered case studies, contributed to Twitter polls, or helped in any other way at all. If it wasn't for all the ideas on Twitter, we would never have been able to 'write' this book.

About the Authors

Lyndsay has been an English teacher for over 20 years, and is Trust-Wide English Lead working across 11 schools. Lyndsay works with SLT and English Departments to provide bespoke CPD, mentoring and coaching and curriculum design, and implements and supports with improvement strategies. Lyndsay is a co-author of '*Succeeding as an English Teacher*', as well as a Senior Examiner for GCSE English Literature, and provides focused CPD for a range of schools on behalf of exam boards. Lyndsay is also an SLE for English and Literacy, a Lead English Expert for AQA, a Fellow of the Chartered College for Teaching, a Regional Lead for WomenEd and governor of a local secondary school. Lyndsay is a passionate advocate for women in education, flexible working opportunities for all and LGBTQ+ visibility in education. Lyndsay can be found on Twitter at @LyndsayBawden.

Jade has been a teacher of English for over ten years, and is a former Head of Department. She is currently working as the Trust-Wide Lead Practitioner for English as well as the Whole-School Lead Practitioner for Teaching and Learning in a MAT, helping to develop curriculum and pedagogy. She is passionate about high expectations for all. She has a range of experience as a Senior Examiner for more than one exam board and has studied Assessment and Examining at MA level at the University of Cambridge. Jade has recently become ELE for a local Research School in addition to being a Fellow of the Chartered College for Teaching, and a Regional Lead for WomenEd. Jade can be found on Twitter at @Jade_Hickin.

Kaley is currently the Head of English and Whole School Literacy lead at a school in Derbyshire, having taught for almost a decade. She runs her own education consultancy, HoDandHeart, providing CPD for teachers and school leaders. Kaley is incredibly passionate about using curriculum and pedagogy as a way to challenge social injustice, as well as the importance of ethical leadership and staff wellbeing, all of which she writes about often via her own blog and for TES. Kaley is studying for a master's degree in expert teaching and is a senior examiner. Kaley can be found on Twitter @HoDandHeart.

Introduction

What does it mean to be a middle leader, and what does it mean to do a good job in that role? These are the questions we aim to address in this book through consideration of research, our combined years of middle leadership, and the experiences of leaders in schools up and down the country. The three of us have seen a lot, and done a lot in middle leadership, from pastoral to curriculum and some of the more undefined bits in between – and honestly, you name a mistake and we have probably made it!

This book has come about from wanting to help others learn from those experiences, the good and the bad, so that you can benefit from our hindsight. The book contains candid case studies of some of the things that can go so wrong, some of the leadership that has brought people to their knees, as well as amazing examples of where people and organisations have got it so right.

Dip in and out of the bits you need and are relevant to you, and remember that to 'do middle leadership right' means to lead with integrity, to hold true to your values and to be kind – to yourself as well as others.

Lyndsay

Education can be a hard field to work in. At the whims of every political change, the teaching profession can be upended seemingly overnight: National Curriculum, Levels, Life without Levels, A-U grades, restorative justice, zero tolerance, 9-1 grades, IGCSE, buckets, Ofsted frameworks, learning styles, direct instruction, global pandemics .... There have to be more changes to teaching than there are in most other professions. And it's exhausting.

Years ago, I remember teaching a lesson in a school to a GCSE class and it being graded Outstanding. I felt pretty great. Eighteen months later I taught the same lesson to a similar class in another school – and everything about it was wrong. Where were my mini-plenaries? Did I know I spoke more than the students? The students were in rows and not groups. The Learning Objectives (LO) wasn't

DOI: 10.4324/9781003160557-1

written on the board! I felt deflated, like a rubbish teacher, and I asked myself the question: where had I gone wrong?

But it wasn't me who had gone wrong; it was the education system, with its ever-changing demands on teachers, fads and snapshot judgements. A system that was, and still is, leading to the burn-out of thousands of dedicated professionals across the country. Professionals whom schools, and the children we teach, cannot afford to lose.

When I received the feedback that my lesson was 'OK, but ...', my confidence was severely dented. I was already taking antidepressants for anxiety and depression, probably related to having had my eldest son but also due to the emotional fall-out of being forced to change my job after maternity leave because I wanted to work part-time. This feedback just added the icing on the cake: I wasn't a good enough teacher.

Luckily, I had a support network around me in the form of my husband, family and some great friends, and they helped me get through it. But others aren't so lucky.

And this is where leadership comes in. I've heard it said that every teacher is a leader, and that's true. But the linchpin of all schools, the glue that holds us all together, is the middle leadership. No initiative in a school, no matter how evidence-informed or good for the students, will succeed if it's not backed by the middle leaders. No team will be effective without a thoughtful, ethical and effective leader in charge.

Those leaders need to shield their team from the 'slings and arrows of outrageous fortune' that hound us in education, and filter out the noise to find the true priorities to help their team thrive and their school improve. Without this, your teachers will be overwhelmed and directionless, and your SLT will be unable to implement their plans for school improvement.

And that, hopefully, is where this book comes in.

Jade

During my time working in education, I have had the good fortune to work with some wonderful leaders who demonstrated compassion, created inspiration and made going to work something that was fulfilling and enjoyable. Two leaders I have had stand out to me. One of them is co-authoring this book, and you will do well to listen to all of her sage advice. The other is sadly now retired, but working with her showed me how someone can professionally hold their team members to account for assessment accuracy, support their teams through crises and always make things better with cake; I cried for days when she retired!

Unfortunately, these magnificent examples have been far outweighed by seeing middle leaders who have been the opposite. And the resulting effects on the teams they have led have been astounding. In one school, with the change in department leader, I witnessed the most heartbreaking disbanding of a happy and collegiate team of professionals as their morale and joy was gradually ebbed away by the new middle leader's inflexible adherence to SLT's decrees, unwillingness to speak up for their team and inability to tackle core aspects of their role such as behaviour management; for example, rather than trying to improve an ineffective school-wide behaviour policy, teachers who stuck religiously to the policy were told to stop using the department detention system because the department head just couldn't cope with the number of students he had to deal with at lunchtime – and he told this to the teachers in front of the classes! In other examples, I have seen teams that blindly follow, with unswerving loyalty, middle leaders who fiercely protect their departments, but fail to apply important protocols that would mean equity, excellence and development; the team's personal interests might be the focus of curriculum decisions, for example, but the knowledge that the students encounter as a result of this is not as robust or well-structured as a result.

I do believe that nobody sets out to do a bad job, so why are these middle leaders getting it so wrong? I think it is a lack of understanding and lack of support. Middle leadership is such a difficult role to fulfil: a balancing act in which you must consider so many different voices and areas, that there needs to be more help to enable these people to do the good job that I am sure they must want to do. I know that when I became a middle leader, as just an Recently Qualified Teacher (RQT), I was desperately underprepared, and there was very little out there to help me to learn the essential things that I needed to know about to do the job well. As somewhat of a perfectionist who hates to get things wrong, and likes supreme clarity over expectations, this was really difficult for me, and I would have been so grateful for something to give me examples, experience, just the feeling of talking to others who had gone through the same thing and could use that to guide me. We all need some friends and colleagues who can say, "This is where I messed up – this is how you should try not to do the same!" That is what this book is meant to be.

So, for the pastoral leaders and heads of department who can see their teams falling apart, the ones who are feeling pressure from those above and around them because they aren't quite getting it right, and those, like I was, who are lonely and lost and just haven't got a clue what they are doing – I hope this book is your helpful friend.

Kaley

Being a teacher is really hard. I don't care what anybody says about 'all those holidays' and 'leaving at 3.30 with the kids'. Those in the thick of education know the truth, and if it was easy in the way that some people make out, we wouldn't be suffering from a retention crisis in our field as I write; in fact, according to research conducted in 2018, 47% of teachers[1] experienced depression or anxiety as a result of work, and that isn't a statistic we can ignore.

Middle leaders have the ability to change that statistic. In a field that's too frequently used as a political football, and where classroom teachers have to take the kicks, we have to employ compassion, humanity and integrity at the core of every leadership decision that we make. Our classroom teachers are our future leaders and, if we treat them as 'human first, professionals second',[2] then we will have teachers who feel valued, and are happy at work. We will have leaders of the future who also treat their teams the same. We can only hope that, if that cycle continues, we will see much fewer concerning statistics about the mental health of our teachers, and that retention and recruitment statistics won't be telling such a bleak story.

In progression towards leadership, you take on board every element of leadership that you experience: the good, the bad *and* the ugly. And sometimes, it's *really* ugly and *really* bad. With each little element of leadership that you experience, you decide what to borrow and what to pop on the shelf – high up, but not out of sight: always there is a reminder of how *not* to lead a team.

My journey towards leadership seemed to happen very quickly; I went from qualifying to Second in Department in a matter of 18 months, and have worked in middle leadership since Second in Department, Head of House and Head of Department, and now the Head of English and Drama with a whole-school leadership responsibility for literacy. In that time, I've worked with a number of other leaders and I've learnt from every single one of them. There are a fair few that stand out more than others, for reasons good and bad: the one who believed in me enough to look into the Assessment Only Route for Qualified Teacher Status (QTS) which I knew absolutely nothing about and then persuaded the Senior Leadership Team (SLT) to fund it for me; the one who told me to 'get [my] game face on' after they found me crying about my recent miscarriage and expecting me in lesson imminently; the one who was power-hungry and seemed to enjoy trampling on everybody else on their way up and the one who taught me the importance of being a positively disruptive voice and to challenge things in a solutions-based way (who also happens to be one of the co-authors of this book!).

Each of the leaders whom I have worked with has made me the leader that I am today, and I continue to learn daily in the hope of being a leader to those in my team who they are not afraid of, who they trust, and who makes them feel valued and important every single day. By no means am I the perfect middle leader, but I like to think that the journey I've been on means that I'm Doing Middle Leadership Right for the most part, though of course we all make mistakes, and fallibility is key to effective leadership too.

If we really think about it, and we look at middle leadership training, are we ever told what to do? In total honesty, for the first few years of middle leadership, I felt like I was there to be a yes wo/man to do as my seniors requested, and I found myself getting frustrated after about six months. There was a significant level of change during my first role as a middle leader, but I often felt more like a personal assistant to the Head of Department than I did a valued contributor to ideas about curriculum and progress. As I moved into pastoral middle leadership alongside curriculum, I felt the same. It was listening to the likes of Emma Turner and Helena Marsh at WomenEd Unconference in 2018, and reading books such as *Lean*

In, Radical Candour, and The Compassionate Teacher that I realised my role as a middle leader was not to sit back and do everything asked of me but also to hold SLT to account and to provide a voice for the people in my team. Have I been labelled 'difficult' and 'outspoken' for doing so? Of course I have! I like to call it positive disruption, personally. More on that later.

This book was written because, in order for a school to be successful and for implementation of initiatives to work, middle leaders have to be on board, and senior leaders should listen to them and value their input. Middle leaders are the engine room of every school, and without them, the machine would simply shut down. Hopefully, this book will empower current and aspiring middle leaders to never, ever be a yes person but to always challenge, to always hold compassion and integrity at the very core and to always insist on the very highest of expectations in order to support those that we are all in education for: our students.

May we lead with our hearts, always.

Notes

1 Teacher Wellbeing Index, 2018.
2 Myatt, https://www.marymyatt.com/blog/humans-first-professionals-second

Ethical leadership and managing change

Surely we've all been there: your boss is lovely but hopeless at making decisions. Or, your boss gets brilliant results but tells you to 'man up' on your first day back after a bereavement: lovely person, crap manager. Hideous person, brilliant at getting results. Is the middle ground the holy grail? This chapter is aimed at helping us attain that elusive balance of high effectiveness and high humanity.

But what is ethical leadership, and what does it mean to be an ethical leader in a school? It can be pretty hard to stay true to your ethics in the face of long hectic days (weeks, months…), and decisions being made under pressured conditions, so in order to establish what this actually means, let's look at the key characteristics of an ethical leader:

Ethical leadership can be defined by the following traits[1]:

1. Justice

2. Respecting others

3. Honesty

4. Humanity

5. Teambuilding

6. Value-driven decision-making

7. Encouraging initiative

8. Leading by example

9. Value awareness

10. No tolerance for ethical violations

But, what does this mean in relation to middle leadership in schools? Let's unpick this further:

DOI: 10.4324/9781003160557-2

Justice

As children, we were sensitive to injustice: when your brother got a larger slice of cake, when you only got 58 minutes on the telly rather than the agreed 60, or when an inferior piece of work was presented to the school in assembly instead of your masterpiece; as an adult our sense of justice is arguably more refined. Being treated justly is tied up in our self-worth and perception of ourselves. As leaders, we need to be just, not just towards others but towards ourselves too. We cannot be seen to have favourites in our teams or to value the opinions of one above another. We must include everyone in our decision-making and fact-seeking. For example: imagine you work in a school team where your department meetings are just for show, or for going through admin; all but one person is in the team WhatsApp group and it's in this group that the important issues are discussed and decided. This is an example of unjust leadership; that team will never function effectively, and the ostracised person will feel undervalued and ignored. In a profession with a recruitment and retention crisis, this is not just morally the wrong way to behave, but it's a pretty poor business decision too. Being just in this situation means deleting the group, or including everyone, or ensuring it's a non-work group, and bringing the decision-making into the formal work meetings where everyone can participate, so there's transparency and fairness in the process.

Respecting others

This means listening to what your team has to say and taking their views into account. It doesn't mean you have to agree with them, or follow their advice, but you do them the courtesy of hearing their perspective. This makes your team feel valued and included and shows that you work collaboratively as a team. When we stepped up to middle-leadership roles, we all discovered that this was difficult due to time – everyone wanted to talk to us and we didn't get any work done! Setting boundaries is crucial in managing this. Saying, can we talk about this after school, or let's schedule a meeting about this later in the week, is important for your sanity and productivity – but you must follow it through and set that time aside. Again, this is not just ethically the right way to behave, it makes good business sense: just because you're the boss doesn't mean you hold all the answers. Your team of professional colleagues will not only have brilliant ideas of their own, but they will bring a valuable alternative perspective, and often a more practical/workable idea, as they are closer to the action in the classroom than many leaders. You are harming the ability of your school to move forward if you don't respect the views of your team – never mind the lack of motivation and value your colleagues will feel if their opinions are not listened to.

Honesty

Those of you who have read 'Radical Candour'[2] will be familiar with the phrase 'ruinous empathy', which describes being so empathetic to someone that you can't say anything construed as negative in case you hurt their feelings. It leads people to avoid giving candid feedback about performance in the mistaken view that being 'nice' is more important than being honest.

Lyndsay can write about this with certainty as she is definitely afflicted with ruinous empathy, or at least has been in the past. But the revelation for her has been that, in being too nice, she's actually damaging people, being a poor leader, and letting down the students and the school.

Here's an example; a colleague comes to you with a resource you know they've spent days working on, but you can immediately see it's not fit for purpose, and asks for your opinion. Lyndsay's (ruinously empathetic) instinct: be nice, tell them it's great, that you appreciate all their work, and thank them for their efforts. They go away feeling happy. But really, who does this help? Perhaps both Lyndsay and the colleague in the short term, as she's given them a verbal pat on the head, dodged a potentially difficult conversation (more on them later!), and made them feel good. Who does it hurt? Everyone: the colleague thinks their work is acceptable, and isn't aware of what or how to improve it, and wastes more of their time doing the same in future. The students in their class suffer as they don't learn the most powerful knowledge in the most effective way, thus wasting precious curriculum time.

The result of this is: you suffer, as the performance of your team is poor. The school suffers, as results don't improve or go backwards. Your relationship with the team, as you're seen as nice but ineffective, and nobody wants a useless manager, no matter how nice they are.

Honesty, plus kindness, is key for the long-term effectiveness of your team, and for all the people in your team individually – and is also the most ethical way to behave.

Humane

Whilst it's imperative to be honest, the way you are honest is crucial. Acting with humanity and remembering that people have feelings is a priority. Deliver news in person where possible, and be clear but sensitive. Give people the respect they deserve by taking time to speak to them one-on-one, and affording them privacy from others when delivering difficult news. For example, publicly criticising a colleague by name in a staff meeting, or as we have experienced, shouting at a member of staff in front of a classroom full of students, is not the action of an ethical leader. Not only is it counterproductive, probably leading to resentment and animosity from the colleague whose behaviour you want to change, it also shows you as lacking in humanity and respect. Leading through fear and humiliation will only take you so far; leading through humanity with ethics will engender loyalty, communication, and productivity.[3]

There are some very practical ways you can ensure that you're being humane in your approach to leadership:[4]

■ Be clear about your feedback: if you are simply giving an opinion, make that explicit; if it's an instruction, use your language accordingly: this is a priority.

■ Be timely: Just because we are working on a Friday night, or Sunday morning, doesn't mean that your team is, or should be. But if you ask them questions or send them actions at these times, it can be easy for them to see that as you expecting them to work then, too. A way around this is to delay-send on emails or to add a clear disclaimer about working patterns and flexibility. Another point on this is to think about the psychological impact of your timing: asking a colleague you manage on a Friday to have a meeting with you on a Monday, without being specific about the content or purpose, might have the unintended consequence of ruining their weekend through worry and stress. Setting deadlines is similar: do not expect your team to have actioned requests over the weekend – they have a life and deserve that downtime – or if they have part-time hours that need to be accounted for in the timeframe. Do not expect or presume that you can directly or by implication take up their time outside of work – this is why we have a hard-won directed time calendar.

■ Make priorities realistic: we can't do everything at once, and to demand so increases stress, as well as the chances of failure. We only have so much cognitive capacity as well as hours in the day. Establish your priorities, and be clear about what you expect and when. Seek feedback on the feasibility of this, and be reasonable. And ensure the *why* of the goal is clear to all – the best teams will have a collective sense of what is important and why, and will row together, and you set the tone for that culture.

■ Give your time equitably: do not give in to having an inner circle, or clique; include everyone. This doesn't mean you can't have friendships, but in work time you have to be seen to be impartial, and actually *be* impartial. This reduces the impression of favouritism and helps you lead more effectively: tempting though it might seem, if you surround yourself with cronies all you will hear is an echo chamber of your own thoughts.

■ Delegate and devolve decision-making: you cannot do everything, and why would you want to? Respect the expertise of your team members and trust them to do the right thing. Give them space to run their own agreed projects and teams, and show that you believe in them by giving them room – physically and virtually – to work. This means that not everything will be 100% successful or as you envisage it – it might be better, or it might fail. But that is a learning experience for them and for you. Showing trust in your team increases their trust in you as a leader. But crucially, you need to be able to judge when you do need to step in, and you need to be available for your team to ask you for support if they need it.

Case Study: Anonymous

I was working in a well-regarded and high-performing school; I was pregnant with my eldest child and in charge of Y11, stepping in for someone who was themself having a very difficult pregnancy and was on bed rest. On my way to school one morning, I skidded on ice and crashed my car. Luckily neither the car nor I were seriously damaged, but I was really shaken up, and very well aware of the precariousness of pregnancy. I booked an appointment with my midwife for some reassurance and called school to tell them I wouldn't be in that day.

On my return the next day, one of my colleagues took me aside; the Deputy Head, on being informed of my absence, said 'call her back and tell her she has to come in'. When told I had been in a car accident, his response was 'Oh right, well that's OK then'.

Not one person from SLT mentioned the crash or asked if I was OK; it was as though it hadn't happened.

So how did this impact me? I was devastated –it brought home to me how nobody on the SLT gave a damn about me, or my baby. It showed me that nobody cared about me as a person –I was just there to get a job done, nothing more. And it also made me 100% determined never to make anyone else feel like that, and to be the exact opposite of those leaders.

When I look back now on the times I have felt frustrated, undervalued, or terrified of yet another public reprimand, they have all been times when leaders have exhibited a lack of ethical leadership.

Teambuilding

Whilst your personal motivations are important, we need to remember that we are striving for a shared goal and that as Aristotle allegedly said, we are greater than the sum of our parts. Working towards a shared endeavour helps people feel connected and gives a sense of community. Teaching can be a very lonely profession, in classrooms as often the only adult all day, and then working on your own to plan or mark, so being a team combats that. Sharing workload e.g. sharing planning, marking work as a team, comparative judgement and consistently holding up behaviour expectations enables a feeling of cohesion and helps your team and therefore the school function more effectively. Even if you, as a middle leader and perhaps an established authority figure, don't need to employ certain behaviour management techniques, modelling those for your team shows that you are working together, as well as showing a united and consistent approach to your students. It's also another way of showing respect to your colleagues, to demonstrate that you don't think that you're above such practices, and that you 'walk the walk'.

In a practical way, team-teaching and sharing planning not only develops people professionally but it can also alleviate any feelings of disconnect or isolation which might build up. And striving together for a common goal supports everyone in feeling valued and important. For example, when writing a new curriculum, it might be 'easier' to write it yourself – after all you are the most experienced teacher on the team, and you're the leader so you know best. But that arrogance will likely lead to an inferior curriculum, a lack of CPD for your team, and a disconnect when your team is teaching units they had no part in developing. Working as a team might take a little longer at the outset, but the benefits vastly outweigh the cost.

Values awareness and value-driven decision making

This underpins almost all of the other characteristics of ethical leadership: establish your values and revisit them regularly, make them the guiding principle behind every decision and action that is taken. Early on in Lyndsay's career as an HoD, she went to a CPD session: How to lead an outstanding English department. Step 1 was: establish a vision and your values. She duly came back to school, thought up a pithy vision statement, popped it on a display board in the office, told everyone about it at the next department meeting, and then promptly forgot about it. That's it, job done. It was never referred to again. And therefore, had no impact on the department. What she needed was for this to be lived and breathed, clear and understandable, and referred to all the time, so it underpinned decision-making about curriculum, CPD, pedagogy, etc. As a leader, your role is to over-communicate those values to ensure that they permeate into everyone's subconscious and that those values are always prioritised.

Your organisation's values need to be at the heart of all the actions taken in your school and influence all your thinking and decisions. When they are clear to you, and clear to all your colleagues, they should drive your leadership: Will this thing improve students' progress? Is it good for staff wellbeing? What other work will we take away in order to facilitate this being implemented? If you are in middle-leadership, it may well be that these values have been cascaded down to you via SLT, but that doesn't mean that you cannot make them your own. For example, your school's values might be: Excellence, Collaboration, Support and Innovation,[5] but what does that actually mean for your team? Let's look at one of these in detail, Excellence, as it seems to be used across many schools and Trusts. We would suggest that you lead a discussion with your team as to what Excellence means for you: is it excellent presentation in books? Is it excellent classroom displays? Is it excellence in GCSE results? Is it excellence in expectations of learning behaviour? Developing and clarifying what these mean for your particular context ensures that there is a clarity of shared meaning in your team, and that those values are then returned to whenever decisions need to be made – they underpin your progression and development as a team.

A further note on values is that it's really important to work for an organisation where your personal values align with those of your organisation; if they do not, you will not believe in what you are doing, being asked to do, and asking of others.

And acting in a way which is contrary to your beliefs is the antithesis of ethical leadership.

Encourage initiative

Nobody likes to be micromanaged; it's disempowering and limiting. Staff who are micromanaged feel frustrated and unvalued, and organisations which encourage this suffer from a lack of initiative and progress, plus seeing higher staff turnover.[6] Whereas when we give our colleagues agency to take risks, to find their own ways of working, and to take ownership of their work, we are empowering them to be professional and signalling that we trust them. We don't want staff to have to wait for instructions, we want them to feel confident about striking out and taking action where needed. The more we encourage this, giving honest feedback and ensuring our values are instilled and understood, the more we show trust in our teams. That's not to say that we leave everyone to their own devices all the time of course! It's a balancing act.

For example, when Lyndsay was first HoD, she only had a line management meeting twice a year – she felt isolated, unimportant, and lost. She had no idea what she was doing and just had to find her own way without the benefit of expert guidance, and she made so many mistakes which could have been avoided. Fast forward two years and she was having weekly line-management meetings, where she was constantly being told what to do: this left her feeling untrusted, insecure and resentful – striking a balance is key. And don't think that you have to decide that balance alone – ask your team what they want; is a weekly meeting enough? Is one each half term too little? Include them in the decision-making process, and be flexible: just because once a fortnight is right for a certain point, it doesn't have to be set in stone.

Initiative from your team allows you and them to get on with their work with confidence and autonomy, and if you have a clear collective goal and vision, and an agreed framework for quality assurance, then you'll be getting the best from your team for the benefit of everyone.

Leadership by example

Walking the walk. If we are asking our colleagues to do something, model it for them, ensure consistency of expectation, and show everyone you're a team. For example, don't reprimand staff for watching videos in the last week of the Christmas term, and then stick YouTube on so you can get your making done (yes, real-life example!). It undermines your colleagues and undermines you. If we say we are going to prioritise staff wellbeing and work-life balance, don't email people at 11.30 pm on a Friday night, don't set deadlines that mean people have to work over a weekend, don't set numerical % performance management targets. If you say something, follow it through and lead by example.

Case Study: Anonymous

I once worked for a school where we were encouraged to support the rest of our department in our PPA time and at lunchtimes by intervening if we heard a noisy class, having students work in the office with us if they needed removing, and sitting with students in classrooms at lunch if it was wet outside. For the most part, people were happy to comply with this, as everyone wanted to help out and be helped in return. Where this fell down was on a Wednesday afternoon, when SLT had their weekly two-hour team meeting, which was sacrosanct. In this department, everyone taught on Wednesday afternoons, so there was nobody on PPA to support with behaviour, and the Head of Department was part of SLT, and so was in the meeting. This meant that Wednesday afternoons were a nightmare; we all dreaded them in anticipation of the poor behaviour we would have to endure with no one to turn to. We repeatedly requested support from SLT during this time, but we were told that we would have to manage ourselves as their meeting took priority. Very quickly, people became disillusioned by this double-standard and reluctant to give up their PPAs and lunchtime to support with behaviour, and that's because it wasn't being modelled by the leadership (and yes I know, the whole behaviour system needed a complete overhaul – but that's another story!).

No tolerance of ethical violations

This sounds easy but can be hard when faced with pressure, both in terms of expecting it from yourself and your team. We all like to think of ourselves as good people who do the right thing, but sometimes the right thing is a little unclear. For example, the pressure for good results in schools leading to the 'extra help' given to students producing their coursework, or teaching to the test instead of the domain. These might seem like sensible or even necessary actions, but again holding the vision and values in mind reminds us of why we are really doing this job: not for league tables or Ofsted ratings, but to make a difference to children's lives, to help them learn, to enable them to be useful and happy members of our society. The ethical violations described above might seem like easy shortcuts, but they fall down when examined in the light of our core values. Our job as leaders is to take the time to stop, step back and evaluate, and uphold the high values of the organisation long-term. And we cannot make an exception to these values, we have to walk-the-walk and model the ethical practice we wish to see in others.

Managing change and ethical leadership

Times of change are often times of stress, and times of stress are when it's easy to let our ethics slip a little in the pressure to act and react and to juggle new concepts. And in education, it's fair to say that we experience a lot of change. Learning to manage this change and still be an ethical leader is not easy, but with conscious practice and deliberate decision making it can be done.

If we take the criteria for being an ethical leader, and apply it to situations of change in education, we can see how it helps us to do the right things for our teams, schools and students:

- Be clear in your expectations
  Set explicit goals and criteria; times of change can be confusing and uncertain, so be the voice of certainty and clarity where you can. So instead of: *I think we'll probably have to re-do our feedback policy at some point this year*, try: *We will discuss feedback options in a department meeting after Christmas, until then please use the existing guidance.*

- Prioritise vision and values
  Keep this in mind when changing what and how you do things; it will be an underpinning rationale for all decision-making and support with clarity for your team. Instead of: *Another new policy on the horizon to change everything we're doing*, try: *We'll be amending this to be more in-line with our vision for excellence in the curriculum.*

- Reasonable timescales
  People need time to think about and digest changes in practice, and time to embed new ways of working. Instead of: *From next week, I want all DO NOWs to be made up of spaced-retrieval quizzes*, try an incremental approach: *In next week's department meeting, we'll be reading some research of the impact of routine spaced retrieval, and we will discuss how we can use this to improve our practice.*

- Consider workload
  If we're putting something in, what are we taking away? In our strive for improvement, it's easy to lose sight of the practical implications of a new initiative or priority, but a good leader must always consider their team's context and workload. Instead of: *From now on we're all attending Tuesday night CPD*, try: *I'd like us to use 30 minutes of each department meeting for CPD on our team areas for development.*

- Seek opinions
  Again, when you're under pressure to make or enact changes quickly, it can be tempting to push ahead and make all the decisions yourself in order to facilitate speed; this is a false economy, as no change will be adopted with integrity and fidelity if people haven't had a say in it. Instead of: *We're dropping hockey from the curriculum next year*, try: *'In the next team meeting, we'll be reviewing the Y8 curriculum and evaluating the success of the outdoor team sports we offer.*

- Encourage initiative
  Don't be intimidated or threatened if someone on your team knows more about a topic than you, goes to a CPD you didn't, or makes a connection you

haven't – embrace and encourage it! Instead of: *I don't think that idea will work here*, try: *Let's put it to the team, and maybe look at a trial pilot project?*.

■ Model the change you want to see
You might feel that because of your relative seniority or experience, that you're exempt from some of the expectations you have of your team; in fact the reverse is true – it's even more important that you harness that seniority and experience to model good practice. Instead of: *I'm going to teach this land erosion unit using these resources I developed 20 years ago, they've always worked for me*, say: *I'd like to try this new approach, would anyone like to look at it with me?*.

Case Study: Jonny Uttley – CEO of T.E.A.L. Trust and co-author of *Putting Staff First*

When discussing ethical leadership with Jonny, he marks two occasions where he believes that really ensured he stayed committed to his place of work, because it was clear that his leader valued him as a human with a family and not just a member of staff in a building without a life outside.

The first occasion was when his daughter was due to attend an induction day, where parents had been invited to enjoy a packed lunch in the school with their children. After requesting this leave, it was granted without question by his headteacher at the time. In addition, Jonny was permitted to take his little girl to her first day at school. These two important milestones are ones that no parents want to miss, and Jonny says that his headteacher saw to it that he wasn't missing out either.

Both of these small acts of humanity and integrity really made him feel valued and Jonny now applies the same principles across all schools in his trust now, as CEO at TEAL. Jonny believes that 'the most important thing for our students is that we have a good classroom teacher **in every classroom**' and if we treat those teachers with integrity and humanity via ethical leadership, then 'we can be sure that good teachers will stick around and that our students will have a much more consistently good experience'.

To conclude, putting people first is at the heart of ethical leadership. Our colleagues and our students are much more than %GCSE results and stats on staff recruitment and retention; they are the beating heart and passionate soul that is at the root of all we do and why we do it: to make the world a better place. And you as a middle leader are in the privileged and crucial position of ensuring the success and happiness of those people.

Top tips for leading ethically and managing change

■ Communicate: talk to your team. Explain rationale and thought process.

■ Be transparent: Only keep things from your team when you have to, in the aim of confidentiality or protecting their workloads.

■ Be inclusive: include everyone in decision-making, and listen to their opinions, especially those that challenge yours – encouraging openness and debate will develop your team and engender trust and openness.

■ Be reasonable: In your expectations, in deadlines, in the way you treat people. Remember that they have their context just as you have yours.

■ Be honest: your team and your school deserve you to tell them the truth, with kindness but clarity.

■ Be fair: Don't play favourites or exclude people, especially those who challenge you the most.

Notes

1 Lemoine, L., 10 Ethical Leadership Characteristics, https://yscouts.com/10-ethical-leadership-characteristics/, y scouts.
2 Scott, Kim, Radical Candor: Be a Kick-ass Boss Without Losing Your Humanity. New York: St. Martin's Press, 2017.
3 Lencioni, P., 2005. The Five Dysfunctions of a Team (2002). *Overcoming the Five Dysfunctions of a Team.*
4 Cornett, L. (2012, 07 18). *How to be a Humane Leader in 7 Surprisingly Simple Steps.* Retrieved from Invincible Career: https://medium.com/invinciblecareer/how-to-be-a-humane-leader-in-7-surprisingly-simple-steps-7ea164e5df9
5 Harris Trust, https://www.harriscareers.org.uk/372/why-work-for-us-4/our-vision-and-values
6 Bielaszka-DuVernay, C., Micromanage at Your Peril, Harvard Business Review, https://hbr.org/2008/02/micromanage-at-your-peril.html, February 2008.

Bibliography

Bielaszka-DuVernay, C. (February 2008). Micromanage at Your Peril, *Harvard Business Review*, https://hbr.org/2008/02/micromanage-at-your-peril.html

Cornett, L. (2012, 07 18). *How to be a Humane Leader in 7 Surprisingly Simple Steps.* Retrieved from Invincible Career: https://medium.com/invinciblecareer/how-to-be-a-humane-leader-in-7-surprisingly-simple-steps-7ea164e5df9

Harris Trust, https://www.harriscareers.org.uk/372/why-work-for-us-4/our-vision-and-values

Lemoine, L. 10 Ethical Leadership Characteristics, https://yscouts.com/10-ethical-leadership-characteristics/, y scouts.

Lencioni, P. (2005). The Five Dysfunctions of a Team (2002). *Overcoming the Five Dysfunctions of a Team.*

Scott, Kim. (2017). *Radical Candor: Be a Kick-ass Boss Without Losing Your Humanity.* New York: St. Martin's Press.

2 Quality assurance: balancing accountability and humanity

For far too many years, data was the primary focus for most school leaders: progress data dominated our working lives, and SLT and middle leaders were often guilty of spending too much time staring at spreadsheets and memorising children as numbers rather than people. Thankfully, in light of much more accessible research on which to inform our practice, and a change in inspection foci, we are moving away from this approach. Rather than focusing on numbers and red, amber and green cells in a spreadsheet (of doom) we find ourselves spending time more wisely looking at curriculum, research-led teaching and learning. This allows us to apply our pedagogical and subject expertise to benefit our students as future adults who will enter the world after school as individuals who have been moulded by the curricula and culture that we provide for them.

For the education profession, this is a really positive move in the right direction. Our pupils are not exam monkeys to simply train and get results to support our schools' performance tables; they are children whose horizons need broadening, whose minds need opening, and whose life chances need furthering as a result of their school experiences. It is, therefore, our moral obligation to ensure that our teaching is quality assured effectively, fairly and within the relevant context, but, no teacher should be reprimanded for missing a data target, no staff member should be penalised if their class falls below the rest of the cohort and no feedback should be feared.

Whilst most schools are thankfully moving away from the days of stand-alone lesson observations and grades to label teachers for the academic year, many schools are still stuck in a rut with policies that focus on judging teachers as opposed to supporting them with their professional development.

The majority of leaders know better than to practise this way now, but *we* must still challenge where that practice does occasionally creep in, and ensure that any

DOI: 10.4324/9781003160557-3

quality assurance processes in place are ones that truly support our teams and – as a result – benefit the students that we teach.

If you work in a school where your SLT set arbitrary policies about marking every x amount of lessons, that use numerical targets for your pay award appraisal, or that still grade teachers on a stand-alone lesson and file this as 'performance management', then as a middle leader it's part of your role to challenge this, to ask for the rationale, and to question it when it isn't adequate, and to advocate for the wellbeing of your team. Performance management processes such as lesson observations, learning walks and book 'looks' should only ever be supportive.

Really, truly, give a damn

A common thread throughout this book is that we should lead with our hearts, whilst also holding our teams to account. In doing so, we build trust because we show our team that we want them to succeed, not just for us but for them as individuals.

The most difficult part of management is establishing a trusting relationship with every member of your team for whom you are responsible. Relationships with our team members, just like relationships with our students, are paramount to success. This is hard because the very hierarchy that comes with being more senior than others in a school context means that people can fear you and your feedback. This is something that all three of us writing this book struggled with when we first took on leadership positions in schools, and was one of the founding issues that made us realise the need for this book.

Relationships with our team members are absolutely key because they determine the fulfilment of our roles as a middle leader, and influence the performance of individuals and teams. Therefore, you must work hard when leading from the middle, to guide your team in a way that supports them in building their trust in you, to show them more than just your professional self. Ask about their weekends, ask after their family members, take an interest in them as human beings.

The most important thing that you can do as a leader is to truly care about them, their lives and their careers.

Setting out your stall

Much like with your classroom behaviour management, where you set your stall out with clear expectations for your students, you must do the same as a middle leader when it comes to introducing performance management procedures to staff. There are still thousands of teachers who experienced the grading of lesson observations, or were judged and put on capability based on one lesson observation. These teachers are likely (even if subconsciously) to still be terrified of the consequences of senior members of staff (be that Heads of Department, Heads of Year, their line managers, senior leadership) even being in their classroom. If you make it clear from the outset that you being in a classroom for any amount of time is not a judgement on their overall practice but to support them in providing relevant developmental tools and resources, then you'll put them at ease. However, you must mean what you say and not just pay lip service to this notion.

Keep your own door open

Equally, if you start with an 'open door policy' for your own classroom, and encourage your team members to 'pop in whenever' in order to see you teach (literally that informally) then you'll find that mutual respect will be established and that the very idea of somebody coming into their classroom will be seen as a much less daunting experience. As a result, what you learn from anything you see in your department's classrooms is likely to be a much truer representation of the everyday reality, rather than 'show lessons' that many teachers still have up their sleeve from the days of one-off lesson observations. Such 'show lessons' tell us as middle leaders very little about the true day in and day outs of the learning taking place within our classrooms.

The bigger picture

There is very little that a stand-alone lesson observation/learning walk/book 'look' can truly tell us about an overall picture of teaching and learning. We have all taught really terrible lessons when, in our heads, it was going to be amazing. And we have all taught truly amazing lessons with very little planning.

The point here is that we must look at the overarching picture in order to truly learn about the developmental needs of our departments and, when we do identify areas for development (which we will; there's always something to learn and improve), we don't just tell the staff that it wasn't good enough. We must guide, coach and provide the relevant time and resources required for this area of development. Telling our team members that something isn't good enough is not good enough leadership.

Be radically candid

Just as telling our staff that their teaching isn't good enough isn't good enough leadership, telling our staff that they have nothing to improve, in order to save their hurt feelings, is also not good enough. It's a fine balance between the two and, as we discuss in our Ethical Leadership chapter, radical candour during our quality assurance processes is absolutely pivotal to succeeding in improving our teams' practice, both as a whole and for individuals. As Kim Scott says: 'It's called management, and it's your job'.[1] We are responsible for the results of our team: good teaching and learning, solid behaviour management resulting in minimum disruption to said teaching and learning, and the effectiveness of a broad and rich curriculum.

Graded lesson observations

The problem with grading lessons (and, effectively, the teachers that teach them) is that every observation becomes a high-stakes test. We all know how students respond to high-stakes testing, and we teachers are no different. We are human beings, and if we sense a threat, then often we don't fare well.

Graded lessons are used to subjectively judge the professional delivering the lesson, with little consideration as to what happened before or after that lesson. The concept of measuring progress within one lesson makes little sense, for many reasons. I recall times from the days of graded lesson observations when I was told that my lesson was 'inadequate' because 'the class didn't reach the objective written on the board'. I was once told that 'the class made progress, but not the progress the L/O said.' It seems ridiculous to write this down now, but this was the norm. There was no consideration about the fact that, because there were misconceptions, I needed to reflect on the spot and support my students with some retaught material.

The purpose of watching our teams teach is to gather a broad picture of what is happening in our department, and one lesson observation for one academic year isn't going to cut it. And, what happens with the paperwork from said lesson observations? Filed in a filing cabinet along with past papers of historic cohorts, popped in teacher files in case of any capability procedures necessary in the future? This, as Freya Odell says 'doesn't help to move teachers forward'[2] and that's literally the point of quality assurance, is it not?

Subjectivity

Who is to say that what observer one sees as a 'good' lesson is truly 'good'? What I think is good and what a colleague thinks is good may be entirely different. Thus, graded lessons are subject to a complete lack of reliability, and are incredibly prone to bias. 'Using Ofsted's categories, if a lesson is judged 'outstanding' by one observer, the probability that a second observer would give a different judgement is between 51% and 78%'.[3]

This lack of reliability, in turn, leads to a culture of one-off performance as opposed to the necessary gradual improvement of individuals within our teams and our teams as a whole. We shouldn't be entering lessons with our clipboards and a tick-box of variables that we believe to be 'good' teaching on a stand-alone basis; this is more about asserting power and hierarchy, rather than guidance and supportive leadership. Just as we shouldn't be assessing students for the sake of a summative assessment point, we shouldn't be observing teachers and grading them. We must use our roles as middle leaders in a formative way in order to make changes and adaptations to the CPD delivered to our teams, to improve the impact of the teaching and learning that takes place within our departments, and to improve outcomes as a result for our students.

Grading for the sake of grading is distracting to the recipient. I remember being fixated on the grade given; anything less than 'good' was upsetting to hear. It damages staff morale to hear that they are 'inadequate' or 'requir[ing] improvement'. When we are told that we aren't good enough, it's so easy to think that snap judgement is a judgement of us as a teacher overall, and not just from one lesson. As middle leaders, we need to encourage our teams to think deeper than just a grade for one lesson; we need to talk about the learning taking place, about the factors that were effective, and about the areas that we must work on to improve. The detail of the feedback is the important matter, and grades deter attention away from that with the obsession of wanting to always be 'good' or that golden ticket of 'outstanding'. Our lessons are so much more than 1–4; they are part of a wider learning sequence, a curriculum journey and a mere snapshot of this in one lesson observation is not telling of the bigger picture. What matters is the holistic picture and lesson observations are a miniscule pixel in all of it.

I remember sitting after school and planning observation lessons for weeks in advance. As soon as I had chosen the class I wanted to be seen with and the time that suited me best, I would chip away at an all-singing, all-dancing lesson to blow my seniors' socks off. Very rarely did they link to prior learning, or build blocks to the next lesson. They were literally a performance for the observer, but put on a show I did: balloons with quotations inside? Check. Jeremy Kyle shows based on poems? Indeed. At the time, I was thrilled to be graded as outstanding and good on many occasions. Now that I look back at those lessons and see that they were literally one-off showpieces with no link to the curriculum sequence at all I can see how incredibly pointless the whole process was. Equally, once you get one or two 'outstanding' grades for lessons, getting anything less is devastating. That pressure to continue performing is all-consuming, and the opportunity to receive genuinely useful feedback in a lower pressure setting is missed.

Remove the grading from teacher feedback in order to build trust, and improve relationships between you as middle leaders and your team members. Doing so encourages teachers to be more receptive to feedback because the grade, far too often and for far too long, was the determining factor for payment progression and teacher appraisal. Such high stakes breeds only fear of middle and senior leaders, resentment and low staff morale.

Effective learning walks

One thing that takes away the fear of learning walks is if those conducting them are present daily: as a middle leader if you 'walk the walk' through corridors, if you pop your head through the door and ask if everything is alright, then your presence is much less intimidating to both your staff and your students – instead you're more likely to be seen as a supportive presence and one who is welcome.

Effective learning walks take place in a number of different contexts, by a number of different staff. Early career teachers conduct learning walks in order to focus on their own professional development needs identified during discussions with their ITT mentor or subject leads, curriculum leaders will conduct learning walks focusing on priorities identified within their academy improvement plans and data analysis, and heads of year or pastoral leaders will conduct learning walks focusing on student motivation, engagement and behaviour and inclusion strategies.

As a middle leader, you need to conduct learning walks in a formative manner if you want them to be effective. Your experience in those classrooms should tell you something that you didn't already know, or confirm something that you thought you knew. There is little point conducting learning walks without prior thought, planning and specific foci. Remember that learning walks are short snippets and you can aim to get around a whole cohort in one lesson; therefore, prioritise one aspect of your departmental improvement plan and gather information with which to adequately feedback in terms of the bigger picture. Learning walks are not for individualised feedback to every team member, unless absolutely necessary.

I think it's incredibly important that it isn't just the curriculum leader or head of year that conducts learning walks, and that the whole team gets to see a piece of the jigsaw. It's likely that you have seconds in departments or assistant heads of year. Include them in the learning walk process, ask them to come into your classroom, and then bring the team together to generate a discussion about strengths, and areas for development. Plan your departmental next steps with them, draw on the strengths within your team to develop others, empower your team members to work with you to collectively respond to learning walk feedback. Agency over autocracy, always.

Lesson planning expectations

Lesson planning is done differently by every teacher, and resources are created and curated differently in every department across the country, and the importance of lesson planning cannot be overlooked.

When I say lesson planning, I do not mean the tedious filling in of starters, main task, mini plenaries, assessment for learning and end plenaries (yawn!), but really effective lesson planning really means the teacher knowing the ins and outs of every one of their lessons, how they fit into a carefully-considered sequence of learning, and how they will deliver each part.

My lesson planning is made up of this: booklet planned as a department for the whole cohort handed out to staff at the start of every term (one for planning purposes, and one for use with the visualiser to show the class), notes and annotations on planning booklet, a small etching in my diary such as P1 Y9 *Diverse Voices: Harlem Nights*. On the surface, it might seem minimal but the thought and detail that goes into every lesson is etched into every annotation that I make, every note on my planning booklet and every knowledge retrieval answer and question that I plan in advance of the lesson in order to address gaps in learning spotted prior, and to build up to the following lesson(s).

If you are fortunate to be in a department where the 'spine of the curriculum'[4] is provided, then this doesn't mean that your team members need not plan their lessons. In fact, quite the opposite. Encourage your teams to plan together (co-planning), to plan in advance for misconceptions and challenges and to be prepared for every lesson. This doesn't mean asking for lesson plans a week in advance of the teaching, because teaching and learning must be flexible in order to move with the needs of the class, but it does mean insisting that teachers know their lessons inside out, prior to teaching them. It's important that you trust your team to do this, but if you happen to notice that this isn't the case, then a great suggestion made on Twitter recently was that, as part of learning walks and book looks/reviews, to ask teachers to provide their planning booklets (or equivalent if you don't have a bookletised curriculum). Not for judgement but to review in line with the teaching and learning witnessed in learning walks and observations, and the student work evidenced in book looks/reviews.

Performance management targets

There are a number of different factors involved in student outcomes, and putting the pressure on teachers and placing the burden of this on their shoulders through numerical performance management targets can be punitive and far too high-stakes. Our students are not BMWs, and we are not car sales-people. Whilst staff should be held accountable for the success of their teaching and learning, putting a percentage figure on this is oppressive, and should be avoided at all costs (Figure 2.1).

Figure 2.1 Twitter exchange re numerical data targets – Balancing Accountability and Humanity – QA.

The problem with numerical performance management targets

Schools, however, are given targets based on national averages and we must strive to meet them as best we can. This external accountability inevitably places senior leaders under pressure to meet these targets, and this is a pressure often passed down to middle leaders to manage. However, to pin the responsibility of numerical outcomes purely on class teachers is unreliable, and likely to be seen as unfair and unjust by many teachers. It will not support the building of trust or staff morale. If numerical targets must be used, then the language surrounding them should be carefully considered in order for teaching staff to not be afraid of missing them. Encourage the use of generalities such as 'strive to', 'aim to', 'work towards' as opposed to imperatives such as 'must meet', 'will meet or 'will succeed in attaining'.

Of course, performance management targets are often seen as necessary for effectiveness, and we must all accept that 'perpetual improvement'[5] is a part of the ever-changing field that is education, or any organisation, but this must be clearly intertwined with the need for professional autonomy, trust, and continuing professional development. The teachers in our classrooms are subject experts, they have spent their lives in becoming the professionals that they are, and we cannot hold over them a percentage of Year 11 students that must meet a grade four as a determiner for their effectiveness as said expert is unfair – It's highly unlikely that that teacher has taken the Year 11 cohort through from Year 7, and nor are they accountable for the host of external influences that affect a students' exam performance, and therefore how can we possibly determine whether or not they progress on the pay scale in the upcoming academic year, based on that?

Numerical performance management targets oversimplify a complex system, and assume that progress is linear. In summary, as Zoe Enser says: it's just 'more nonsense that distorts teaching'[6] and it forgets that the child is a person rather than a number. Our energy as teachers should never be focused on the data, and should always be on the students.

As a middle leader, you can feedback to your SLT on the effectiveness of numerical targets on your team, and suggest alternatives for them to consider such as more general targets about teachers' contributions to the wider departmental/year group/school target, for a more team-focussed approach which doesn't put pressure on classroom teachers alone.

Marking policies

Feedback is really important to improving progress, and this is true for teachers as well as students, however the traditional notion of marking as the main way to give feedback to students is problematic. The word 'marking' itself is simplistic; it suggests that we simply make a mark on the paper, when in fact research has shown that written feedback on students' books has very little impact on improving their performance. 'Some forms of marking, including acknowledgement marking, are unlikely to enhance pupil progress'.[7] Instead, more fluid forms of formative assessment where the teacher acts on the findings are in fact more effective because 'Pupils are unlikely to benefit from marking unless some time is set aside to enable pupils to consider and respond to marking'.[8]

The arbitrary nature, therefore, of a marking policy that stipulates that teachers must 'mark' books/student work every x amount of lessons, is a pressure unlikely to reap rewards. We have all seen those policies: teachers must tick a page every two weeks; teachers must acknowledgement mark by writing a comment such as 'good work' every eight lessons; teachers must correct spelling and punctuation in every first paragraph on the second Monday of every month.... And how many of us have given up our evenings and weekends to do this, only to find that the students never look at it again? In a profession with a recruitment crisis, these workload pressures are issues we need to be more aware of than ever.

There are still so many schools out there that are still stipulating such rigid approaches to 'marking', but there is another way. Instead of suggesting that teachers mark every x amount of lessons, consider when is the appropriate time for teachers to give feedback on student work. This may differ from class to class, and some may wish to do it more frequently than others. It may also look differently to the traditional model of 'marking' where a teacher makes a comment in a different coloured pen. My team hasn't 'marked' a single book this year. Instead they have provided feedback in a formative way, using a consistent approach used by every person in the department.

By not adding teacher writing on top of student work, but instead providing useful and relevant feedback on how to improve by linking prior learning to future learning, by applying improvements to new contexts, and by revisiting/reteaching previously misconceived ideas, students respond in a way that supports their progress, and teacher time is used more effectively.

Of course, we have to ensure that teachers are looking at student work, otherwise how will we be able to ensure that students are independently applying their learning? However, this doesn't need to be on a specified schedule. Rather than stipulating that teachers mark every x amount of lessons, specify waymarkers where teachers assess student progress and provide formative feedback in order to accelerate the learning. Instead of criticising teachers who haven't 'marked' all 120 of their students' books in the timeframe given, provide CPD on question level analysis, whole class feedback, low-stakes quizzing, or using mini-whiteboards, for example.

Policies that increase workload, instil fear of being 'caught out', and have little impact on student experience or outcomes, need to be eradicated. As middle leaders, you're in a powerful position to ensure that such autocratic demands are phased out, and in their place are policies that support staff wellbeing and student development.

How to conduct book looks/reviews effectively

First thing is first: never, ever use the term 'book scrutiny'. The word 'scrutiny' itself derives from the Latin for 'to search for rubbish'…. I think I've said enough on that matter! (Figure 2.2).

There are a variety of very valid reasons for reviewing books, ranging from an area of concern identified during quality assurance processes, to how a particular demographic of students are performing in relation to their peers. In order to conduct a book look/review effectively, you must first ask the questions: why am I proposing this? What am I trying to find out about?

It's important to ensure that your focus is consistent and specific across your other quality assurance processes at the time they are conducted. This allows you to create a thread of comparison across a range of evidence collated and curated from all elements of the QA.

Many schools conduct separate book looks/reviews to learning walks/observations. This works because it allows a more concentrated focus on the work in front of you, as well as the time and space needed to look at the student work in detail. However, the issues with this are that you can't often interpret the student's work in relation to progress without the teacher or pupil articulating alongside it. An alternative to this is to conduct the book looks/reviews as part of the learning walks and observations or use departmental time to conduct a book look as a whole department.

By conducting book looks/reviews simultaneously to learning walks, you are able to ask students questions about the work and that articulation can support you as the middle leader in understanding the process of learning that has taken place. It also allows you to see how knowledge has been retained over time, and student voice alongside student work is invaluable to learn about the teaching and learning within your department.

By conducting book looks/reviews as a whole department, you remove the (often unspoken) fear of 'us vs them' for your classroom teachers, you invite those without leadership responsibility to see the wider school picture, and you allow every member of your team (including yourself) to learn from others. This is empowering and shows that you value their thoughts and input, regardless of their experience or place in the school hierarchy.

When requesting books, it's important that you specify which students' books you wish to see and that you give your team enough time to gather and bring the

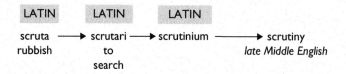

Figure 2.2 Etymology of 'scrutiny' – Balancing Accountability and Humanity – QA.

books to you, but not enough time for them to feel that they have to go back through and 'check that books are marked'. I say this from experience: as an RQT, if I knew about a book 'scrutiny' a week in advance, I waved goodbye to my weekend and spent time back marking that set of books instead of spending time with my loved ones. This is not dissimilar to the point made earlier about the need for book looks/observations/learning walks, etc to be a true representation of the daily goings-on of your department.

Top tips for balancing accountability with humanity

- Always have a focus on quality assurance processes.

- Show that you care, and mean it.

- Use the quality assurance process as a means for piecing together all elements of the jigsaw: 'the big picture'.

- Empower and autonomise your team to work with you in quality-assuring.

- Be present in classrooms frequently so it becomes the norm and not threatening.

- Punitive, arbitrary measures such as numerical performance targets, graded lessons observations and insisting on marking every x amount of lessons, are unlikely to be effective.

- Challenge high-stakes policies, and replace them with formative opportunities.

- Provide autonomy, candid feedback and build relationships.

Notes

1 Scott, 2017 Radical Candour.
2 https://twitter.com/FreyaMariaO/status/1428443411351281668
3 Coe, 2014 Classroom Observation: It's Harder than you Think.
4 Laura Rowlands (@TillyTeacher) via www.hodandheart.co.uk A Bookletised Curriculum.
5 Damien Page, 2014.
6 https://twitter.com/greeborunner/status/1428475512138125316
7 EEF Marking Review, 2016 https://educationendowmentfoundation.org.uk/public/files/Presentations/Publications/EEF_Marking_Review_April_2016.pdf
8 EEF Marking Review, 2016.

Bibliography

Coe, Robert. (2014). "Classroom observation: it's harder than you think." *Centre for Evaluation and Monitoring*, https://www.cem.org/blog/414. Accessed 10 7 2021.
EEF. "Marking Review."*Education Endowment Fund*, https://educationendowmentfoundation.org.uk/public/files/Presentations/Publications/EEF_Marking_Review_April_2016.pdf.

HoDandHeart. (2021). *A Bookletised Curriculum: Laura Rowlands and Kaley Riley. HoDandHeart,* https://hodandheart.co.uk/product/a-bookletised-curriculum-with-laura-rowlands-and-kaley-riley/.

Page, Damien. 2016. "Understanding performance management in schools: a dialectical approach." *International Journal of Educational Management, 30*(2), p. 7. *Leeds Beckett,* https://eprints.leedsbeckett.ac.uk/id/eprint/2228/1/Understanding%20PM%20in %20schools%20-%20author's%20accepted%20version.pdf.

Scott, Kim. (2017). *Radical Candor.* Pan Macmillan.

3 Difficult conversations (how to have them, and not cry)

Giving feedback is an important part of being a middle leader, as you are in a position to see the implications of poor practice at a classroom as well as department and school level. And if you're not honest in your dealings with people, they will ultimately lose respect for you, and you will be unable to do your job effectively. The creation of psychological safety in your team – where honest feedback is valued because it is professional and not personal, and disagreements are productive and not punitive, is the responsibility of the leadership – that is, you. Your leadership creates those conditions for your team to feel safe and respected and therefore to value feedback on their performance as it leads to better outcomes for the shared endeavour of the school: to improve the lives of your students.

Creating that culture is not a quick process, and if you are working in a toxic school or have had a negative previous experience, interpersonal fear can be hard to overcome, as trust takes time to build. But you will not create a culture of psychological safety by not giving honest feedback when it is needed – that is an avoidance of accountability, and a pervasion of low standards, and is one of the reasons that teams fail to operate effectively.

In Lencioni's influential study on team dysfunction, trust, or *lack* of trust, is found to be the foundation of team dysfunction[1]; trust is personal and organic, and without it you cannot build excellent performance, because safe conflict is needed for growth and innovation. And trust comes from respect, truth and honesty, and that sometimes involves having difficult conversations – leading them, as well as receiving difficult feedback yourself with professionalism, and modelling how to act on such honesty.

DOI: 10.4324/9781003160557-4

Case Study: Lyndsay

For years in my career, and if I'm honest in life in general, I have shied away from having difficult conversations. It has gone hand in hand with a lack of self-confidence and self-esteem, both personally and professionally. While I learned to build up confidence in my personal life, work was a different matter, and particularly after coming back from maternity leave, I was really nervous of confrontation and disagreements.

This has not served me well, nor has it served well the people working with me. Because I tried so hard to avoid tough conversations, I let stuff slide, rather than confronting it and dealing with it. This meant I wasn't giving honest feedback to people who needed it, meaning their performance wasn't improving. This in turn impacted on the organisation I was working for, and the students we taught. And essentially it was because of my cowardice.

I'm not even sure where this fear came from; perhaps from being socialised, as many women are, to please, and be kind, in order to be accepted and liked; perhaps from my own sensitivity to criticism —taking it personally and letting any 'negativity' affect my self worth? I doubt I will ever be able to trace the roots of this feeling, but I know now that it's never too late to challenge this perception in yourself, and to become a better leader because of it.

As I have become more senior at work, I have had to be brave and have difficult conversations, sometimes with people who were very difficult. And, at first, this caused me lots of anxiety, lying awake worrying about it the night before, and lying awake dissecting it afterwards. Calling my husband and friends and seeking reassurance. But the more I have done it, the easier it has become. Partly, this is because I have become better at depersonalising these conversations, but it is also because I have also become better at identifying my core values and principles; and if you work for an organisation where your principals align, then if you act in accordance with those then you can never go far wrong in being effective at your job and being true to yourself, which is ultimately what helps us to sleep well at night because we can rest easy knowing that we are doing leadership right.

As well as being sure of my values and principles, another game-changer for me was discovering Radical Candour; this book and associated podcasts opened my eyes to how I was letting myself and my team and my employers down every time I did not address something difficult because I was scared. It helped me to reflect on why I was scared – what exactly would happen?

The realisation was that I didn't want to hurt people's feelings, or as the book would term it I was being 'ruinously empathetic'. I was so scared of upsetting someone —and the resulting tears/anger/disappointment this would engender that I avoided doing it all together or couched my feedback in such vague or positive phrases that it would go largely unnoticed. A 'praise sandwich' was a favourite of my avoidance techniques – sneaking in some criticism in the middle of loads of praise, in the hope I wouldn't have to discuss it or deal with it.

I told myself it was ok to act like this because I was taking the other person's feelings into account —and look at what a good person I was! How lovely I was! But actually, I was not a lovely person, or a good person, I was disingenuous, a placater, a fraud – letting everyone down for short-term avoidance.

As a leader, it's imperative that we develop others and – by avoiding difficult conversations – I was doing the opposite.

Working as a team

To establish psychological safety, and therefore a climate of accepting honest and 'difficult' conversations professionally, your team development needs to be considered. A useful activity to do with your team might be the Trust Ladder, or Cog's Ladder,[2] to evaluate where you are as a team in terms of trust, and consider what you need to move to next steps:

Cog's ladder stages:

1. Polite stage: getting to know each other, seeking approval

2. Why are we here: understanding goals and roles

3. Power: competitiveness, criticism, disagreements

4. Cooperation: working together to achieve goals, listening

5. Esprit de Corps: synergy, trust, respect, caring, openness.[3]

Using this can help you to identify how trusting you are as a team, and also how you increase that trust in order to be able to be honest with each other which in turn improves performance. Teams can and do move naturally through this ladder but as a middle leader your role is to facilitate the team moving to the optimum area – esprit de corps – as quickly as possible.

Cog's Ladder:[4] (Figure 3.1)

In the polite phase, your team will be new and cautious about upsetting anyone or being disruptive; in stage two 'why are we here', the focus moves to team goals and shared objectives to guide behaviour and priorities; in the power phase, competing for power emerges – while it might be your instinct to step in here it's an important step in establishing team roles, so try to let it play out; in the cooperation phase, the hierarchy has now been established and all members should be contributing in different ways to work towards the shared goals; the final phase is the goal of seamless and productive working where the team is effective and productive.

Undertaking this activity alone as a leader or more powerfully as a group allows you to consider team roles and understand and overcome barriers to team performance, thus leading to a more productive working environment where honest and professional feedback as the norm can flourish.

Remember this scenario from the Ethical Leadership chapter:

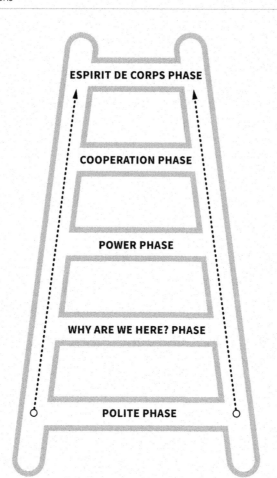

Figure 3.1 Cog's Ladder.

A colleague comes to you with a resource you know they've spent days working on, but you can immediately see it's not fit for purpose, and asks for your opinion. My (ruinously empathetic) instinct: be nice, tell them it's great, that you appreciate all their work, and thank them for their efforts. They go away feeling happy. But really, who does this help? Me and them in the short term, as I've given them a verbal pat on the head and dodged a potentially difficult conversation (more on them later!). Who does it hurt? Everyone: the colleague thinks their work is acceptable, and isn't aware of what or how to improve it, and wastes more of their time doing the same in future. The students in their class suffer as they don't learn the most powerful knowledge in the most effective way, thus wasting precious curriculum time. You suffer, as the performance of your team is poor. The school suffers, as results don't improve or go backwards. Your relationship with the team, as you're seen as nice but ineffective, and nobody wants a useless manager, no matter how nice they are.

In the example above, the honest and ethical action is to be truthful with your colleague; thank them for all their hard work, but explaining what is wrong with what they have done. This will be great CPD for them, as well as ensuring that the quality of their work is of a high standard. Even better if you use this to reflect on your leadership: did you give clear parameters for the work? Were you modelling what you are expecting of your team? If you find this difficult, remind yourself of the bigger picture: what we are aiming for is the best for the students and staff in the school; being dishonest in this situation is not the best for either of them, it's simply you giving into cowardice.

Case Study: Laura Webb, Head of English

My biggest fear in any career has been difficult conversations. I think this is amplified in teaching; being in a classroom is such a personal experience, and we pour our hearts into our jobs, which makes it so difficult to speak to someone about their performance. I have avoided these conversations, but no one wins in this situation – the problem continues and I carry on being stressed about it. I find talking to people about marking is particularly difficult, as I am an experienced examiner and can see when a mark is outside of tolerance, but a lot of English teachers struggle with marking. When I have had to speak to staff about their marking, I have always spoken about the conversation with my line manager beforehand, running through scenarios and what I plan to say. This gives me a little more confidence entering the conversation – just a little!

I've found with some difficult conversations it helps to have tangible examples, so that the person you are speaking to can see what is happening as a result of their choices. So with marking conversations, I always make sure to have the response in front of me. In a conversation last year, I constantly returned to the student's work, and a situation I had been avoiding for a long time was over in ten minutes, with progress made! I think the most anxiety around these conversations is actually in the build-up, worrying about what will happen, but actually having them is easier than people think – everyone wants to get better, and no one wants to be bad at their job! As with everything, practice makes perfect, and the more conversations I have had, the easier it has become, and less fear appears in the build up!

The psychology of difficult conversations

You won't always need to give feedback to someone in an atmosphere of psychological safety; there will be times when you are out of your comfort zone and you worry about how to give a difficult message, or how it might be received.

Recent research has focussed on the tension between wanting to be honest but also wanting to be kind, and, reassuringly, has found that those giving the feedback tend to overestimate the potential conflicts associated with the situation, '*By focusing on the short-term harm and unpleasantness associated with difficult conversations, communicators fail to realize that honesty and benevolence are actually compatible in many cases. Providing honest feedback can help a target to learn and grow, thereby improving the target's overall welfare'.*[5]

Part of the reason we fear giving negative feedback and having difficult conversations is because we know how it can feel to be on the receiving end. Negative feedback can manifest itself as a psychological threat, which can have both behavioural and physical consequences, and we have all reacted to this feedback ourselves by feeling depressed or demotivated or downright angry (just me?). What the research shows is that it is the *way* the information is delivered which is key to mitigating this threat reaction and enabling people to move into a zone where they can act on it constructively and use it to improve performance. The key, according to research, is to mitigate this with wider validation of people's value and importance to an organisation – essentially, making people feel valued.[6]

So how do we have these conversations if we are scared or intimidated? The CORE model[7] can be helpful for us to understand why people might react in certain ways to difficult conversations, and therefore help us plan to mitigate those reactions, in ourselves and others.

Certainty – what we know about the future.
Options – do we have choices?
Reputation – our social ranking.
Equity – are we being treated fairly?

These elements work together in our unconscious to create the reactions we exhibit, positive or negative. Because it is unconscious, these decisions are made almost instantaneously when presented with a situation, so as effective leaders we need to ensure we have considered them before we tackle a situation. Knowing these drivers helps us to consider how to approach difficult conversations in ways which will appeal to these CORE elements, rather than threaten them.

Using the CORE model, here are some tips to ensure you are appealing to these unconscious decision-making factors in ways which will help you get the outcome you need:

Certainty: Set clear goals, enable open communication, share information, break projects down into small steps.
Options: Give choices, facilitate autonomy, create guidelines not rules, define details as a team.
Reputation: Give praise and recognition where it's due, keep negative feedback private, provide learning opportunities.
Equity: Be transparent in decision-making, explain context and actions, be consistent and unbiased in applying policies and assigning work.[8]

How to have a difficult conversation

Knowing the theory and psychology behind how we react is helpful, but sometimes we need more practical strategies too. Before you have that difficult conversation, you might have been dreading or putting off, consider the following strategies:

■ Be specific and give examples: This helps the person understand precisely what you are talking about and avoids confusion and misunderstanding.

■ Know the outcome: what do you want the person to do/think next? Or are you open to ideas on moving forward? Be clear on the outcome you both agree at the end of the conversation.

■ Act professionally: Keep calm, keep your voice level, maintain eye-contact and open body language. Do not ignore tears, offer a tissue and offer a time out.

■ Choose the time and place carefully: Is your office too intimidating? Is there appropriate neutral ground you can use? And do not build up tension for a difficult conversation by emailing on a Friday about a meeting on a Monday – it will heighten anxiety for both of you. Have the meeting on the Friday – rip the bandage off.

■ Be direct: Keep your opening language clear and to the point – like an essay thesis sentence. This helps you get to the point more easily, and ensures you address the issue at hand rather than dodge it.

Case Study: Anonymous

I had a new teacher join my department at Easter 2021 (mid-pandemic!) to cover maternity leave. The teacher leaving had been teaching from home since February half term with a cover-supervisor in the room.

The new teacher came in pretty hard on the classes as behaviour and expectations had, unsurprisingly, slipped in the time their teacher had been delivering lessons remotely. The school I work in is not the kind of place that is used to very strict teachers who demand respect and much is done through relationships and parental contact. (This is changing, slowly, and I don't agree with the current, inconsistent attitude to some behaviour.) Some parents alleged the use of language that was very negative and could be seen as close to bullying certain groups of students. I also had reports from other members of staff of a negativity from this teacher and stories of how she would "rant" about classes.

I met with the teacher when we were both free and chose specific quotes from parental complaints to put to her. She sat meekly listening and took it very hard. She did put her side across and acknowledged that some of her language could have been perceived as negative and I pushed the "perception" being important. She is a very experienced teacher who has held leadership roles in the past. I had been burned by similar complaints about another teacher the year before which had escalated to some much nastier language because I'd let it go too long.

She was very upset after our conversation and was subdued for the next day. I realised my mistake as she clearly took this a lot more to heart than the previous teacher. On top of that, her lessons were excellently planned and the atmosphere in most of her lessons was very calm and productive.

Twenty-four hours after the first conversation, I sought her out to apologise for the way I had shared the concerns initially. We had a very positive conversation about the behaviour policies in the school and how she could use them to snuff out the more argumentative students earlier and I arranged some meetings with key students, parents and heads of years to move things forwards. This is what I should have done in the first instance: find out how much of our school policies she understood and used rather than jumping on the poor choice of language when she was stressed.

Top tips for having difficult conversations

- Practise: have a loved one or friend rehearse the conversation with you. Write down key words or phrases you want to say. This will bolster your confidence and help you to clarify your thoughts.

- Be immediate: don't let it fester: as we know from research on feeding back on students' work that for it to be effective it needs to be immediate. Addressing things quickly stops misconceptions being embedded and minimises any potential damage, and also stops you from having time to fester on it and build it up into a giant obstacle in your head.

- Gain perspective: how much will this conversation you're scared of having matter in a day/month/year? How much will it matter if you don't have it?

- Be the change you want to see: if part of the reason you worry about these conversations is people's defensive reactions then model good practice: ask for honest feedback and be receptive to it. Show others it's ok to get things wrong and to have it told to you so you can improve, and do so with good grace.

- Shift the culture: embed feedback into your ways of working at every level, to allow it to become the norm in your organisation. This moves these conversations from something to be afraid of to something to look forward to as a way of helping improve each others' performance. This can be done through surveys, 1-1s, written evaluations, casual conversations – just make sure that it happens, as it will gather momentum.

Notes

1 Lencioni, P., 2005. *Overcoming the Five Dysfunctions of a Team: A Field Guide for Leaders.* s.l.: Pfeiffer Wiley.
2 Charrier, G. O. (1972). "Cog's ladder: A model of group growth." *SAM Advanced Management Journal* (00360805), *37*(1), 30.
3 Charrier, G. O. (1972). "Cog's ladder: A model of group growth." *SAM Advanced Management Journal* (00360805), *37*(1), 30.
4 Image by David Goodwin.
5 Levine, E. E., Roberts, A. R., & Cohen, T. R. (in press 2019). Difficult conversations: Navigating the tension between honesty and benevolence. Current Opinion in Psychology [To be published in special issue on Privacy and Disclosure, Online and in Social Interactions]. pp. 14.
6 Berinato, S. "Negative Feedback Rarely Leads to Improvement." January–February 2018, *Harvard Business Review*, pp. 32–33.
7 Hills, J. Minimise threat and maximise reward to accelerate change, HR Zone, https://www.hrzone.com/perform/business/minimise-threat-and-maximise-reward-to-accelerate-change#:~:text=We%20created%20the%20CORE%20model,in%20social%20situations%2C%20like%20work December 2018.
8 Hills, J. Minimise threat and maximise reward to accelerate change, HR Zone, https://www.hrzone.com/perform/business/minimise-threat-and-maximise-reward-to-accelerate-change#:~:text=We%20created%20the%20CORE%20model,in%20social%20situations%2C%20like%20work December 2018.

Bibliography

Berinato, S. (January–February 2018). "Negative Feedback Rarely Leads to Improvement." *Harvard Business Review, 1*, pp. 32–33.
Charrier, G. O. (1972). "Cog's ladder: A model of group growth." *SAM Advanced Management Journal* (00360805), *37*(1), p. 30.
Hills, J. (December 2018). Minimise threat and maximise reward to accelerate change, *HR Zone*, https://www.hrzone.com/perform/business/minimise-threat-and-maximise-reward-to-accelerate-change#:~:text=We%20created%20the%20CORE%20model,in%20social%20situations%2C%20like%20work
Lencioni, P. (2005). *Overcoming the Five Dysfunctions of a Team: A Field Guide for Leaders.* s.l.: Pfeiffer Wiley.
Levine, E. E., Roberts, A. R., & Cohen, T. R. (in press 2019). Difficult conversations: Navigating the tension between honesty and benevolence. *Current Opinion in Psychology* [To be published in special issue on Privacy and Disclosure, Online and in Social Interactions]. pp. 14.

4 Curriculum development: the theory

Unless you are very new to the education sector, you will not have failed to notice the increased usage of the word 'knowledge' in the educational lexicon. Whether accurate or not in its application, there is no escaping the increased focus on knowing, and on the content of the curriculum. Of course, we want to ensure that we are using 'knowledge' accurately, wisely and with fidelity. As a middle leader of curriculum, your role in ensuring that this happens is paramount; recent Ofsted research defined a 'knowledge-rich' approach as one in which curriculum leaders are clear on the 'invaluable knowledge they want their pupils to know'.[1]

If a curriculum isn't working, or if it is only working for those from more advantaged backgrounds, then this needs addressing. Michael Fordham tells us, 'A curriculum is too frequently understood to be simply a list of things to learn and indeed, by some definitions, that is all it is'.[2] And this is where we often go wrong – a set of skills, or even facts, is not a curriculum. We need to think about how it all works together and in order. As Fordham continues, 'Curriculum [has] a temporal dimension: it [does] not just set out what [is] to be learned, but [provides] a sequencing to that'.[3] So, we need to think about our curriculum in terms of progression – where and when we are within what we are learning determines the progress: 'A curriculum sets out the journey that someone needs to go on to get better at the subject'.[4]

This chapter will break down all the curriculum vocabulary and theory that you will need to develop your knowledge-rich curriculum, and then we will deal with the practicalities that follow.

This is something that cannot be summed up in a simple statement or definition. One foundation of the concept is ED Hirsch, starting with his 'Cultural Literacy: What every American Needs to Know'[5] which gives an outline of the very content that is considered by Hirsch to be important in achieving knowledge equality across the many social divides and actively participate in modern society. A key development to this is the work of Michael Young, who harnessed the idea of powerful knowledge. The EEF points out that the recent Ofsted research and

                                           DOI: 10.4324/9781003160557-5

focus means essentially that schools must make choices about what to prioritise, and that this echoes Michael Young's famous emphasis on 'powerful knowledge' and runs through many recent articles and blogs.[6] Young is less prescriptive about the actual content of powerful knowledge than Hirsch had been, but, through also revisiting and refining this idea and the power that knowledge holds, champions the role of subject disciplines in selecting, refining and curating, their own area of powerful knowledge.[7] As the leader of your subject, you are the leader of this process, and this is both the foundation and the pinnacle of your role: it is a gift and a huge responsibility to conduct what your students learn, and when.

The shift to a focus on knowledge is important. When we shift our focus, as curriculum leaders, to knowledge, it means that we are focusing on the content and substance of our students' education rather than their experience in the classroom; what we teach matters. It means that we are championing our subject disciplines, and trying to give our students the truth at the heart of them which we believe to be their entitlement as members of our society. This is how we achieve equity of experience, understanding and opportunity.

Case Study: Anonymous, Head of Department

When I became a Head of Department, the department I inherited had seen its GCSE results decline for each of the previous three years. Fast-forward a few years, and my department had reversed this trend. We had seen students' results improve three years in a row. But when my team and I were analysing results, something still didn't feel right. There was a mismatch – the time and effort we were investing were only yielding marginal gains for our students. To me, students' results were marginally improving in spite of what we were doing, not because of what we were doing. What were we doing wrong, and how could we get better?

I began unearthing the answers to these questions and many more when I discovered cognitive science. Almost immediately, it was apparent where we had been going wrong – we had developed bad habits. VAK had long gone, but when I look back and recall how we were doing practice exam questions in KS3, I feel a sense of shame.

Put crudely: our KS3 curriculum had become nothing more than a diluted version of our KS4 curriculum. And our KS4 curriculum wasn't much more than the GCSE specification. We had this notion that if we finished teaching the specification by Christmas of Year 11, we would have five or six months of revision time. In reality, we spent five to six months reteaching our students because they couldn't remember much of what we had been teaching them. Our curriculum was a mere list of discrete facts; we were unknowingly focussing on task completion over knowledge acquisition. We were using levelled outcomes and believed that differentiation meant setting different activities for students based on their predicted grades.

I suspect what I have described so far sounds like a nightmare. But it wasn't all doom and gloom. I've never been precious and consider myself a positive recipient of feedback. Most of the habits I had developed weren't of my own doing; they were reflections of the poorly conceived and misunderstood policies that still permeate our education landscape.

Our move to a knowledge-rich curriculum began by reading the work of Michael Young, Mary Myatt, Tom Sherrington, Mark Enser and engaging with our relevant subject associations. We learnt about interleaving and spacing and the importance of paying attention to the core and hinterland. The A-Level Content Advisory Board (ALCAB) subject report gave us a better understanding of the concepts taught beyond KS4. These reports are helpful, as they make explicit the knowledge your students need to acquire to study your subject beyond KS4. The ALCAB report helped my department identify the core concepts that act as the underlying organisational structure for our curriculum. These concepts frequently appear in KS3 and KS4, providing containers for which to store new knowledge.

Today, department meetings afford fruitful collaboration. Our meetings are less administrative; we spend time developing subject knowledge, pedagogy and refining our curriculum. Challenging work no longer means answering exam questions in KS3; it means developing cultural capital through reading domain-specific texts and having the knowledge to question the validity of theories and models. We now consider how best to boost memory through retrieval practice and the use of prior knowledge. Activating prior knowledge makes it more probable for students to forge links; the rich associations of our subjects are made apparent.

This is a very brief account of my transition to a knowledge-rich curriculum. Here is a summary of my recommendations:

1. *Engage in the latest discussions about curriculum design. Invest time in engaging with experts of repute in your subject area and any subject-specific associations.*

2. *Dedicate department time to developing subject knowledge, pedagogy and refining the curriculum —curriculum work should never be considered finished.*

3. *Make reading central to your curriculum design. Select texts that are challenging and help students make sense of the importance of what they are learning.*

4. *Teach beyond the specification. Don't be scared to go off-piste and explore the hinterland.*

5. *Give your subject the love and respect it deserves. Your subject is about so much more than preparing students for an exam. Don't ever apologise to students that what they are about to learn is dull or difficult. Celebrate the challenge and explain why they are learning it. If you aren't passionate about what you are teaching, why should your students be?*

What knowledge-rich means to you as a curriculum leader

Putting your knowledge-rich curriculum in place is not an easy process, but it certainly can be enjoyable and rewarding.

As a middle leader, you may be facing several challenges to your vision of a knowledge-rich curriculum, from both above and below. If you are lucky enough to already be working in a school in which there is a genuine understanding of a knowledge-rich approach to curriculum, then your job will be much easier; you will be helping to harness this concept within your subject discipline, using your, and your team's, expertise in this area to develop the specific content of your curriculum area. But what if you are not working in one of these schools? Then you are going to have to do some careful work to show your SLT what this approach really is, and why it is effective. And either way, you are probably going to have to win over at least some of your team. The way to do this is through research – carefully selected and presented research that will prove the relevance and effectiveness of this approach, drawn from a range of sources, including, dare we mention it again, Ofsted, who can be particularly persuasive for a lot of SLT! Collaboration is also a powerful tool: as your team realises that this is something that is being done with them, not to them, and that their expertise as subject specialists is valued, they will feel increasingly empowered by the reconnection with the subject that they love.

In developing your curriculum, you need to be prepared for the amount of time it is going to take: one INSET day to rewrite is far and away from an adequate amount of time. Your curriculum will have to be built gradually. Of course, results are important and there is always a lot of focus on the examination years, and this may encourage you to start by looking at these key stages as the place to start your curriculum revolution. At Key Stage 4 and Key Stage 5, there is usually a level of dictat in the form of exam specification which must be adhered to, but this will most often contain broader concepts, texts, ideas that need to be honed down to the specific content that you believe your students need to know in order to show their success in the final assessment. However, more important are the building blocks towards these years, as these will form the basis on which this more complex knowledge will be built upon. Just like an architect needs a detailed plan of the building they are creating before they start laying those foundations though, it is important that we have a clear overview of the whole curriculum so we know where we are heading. So, lay out your framework: what is the core knowledge that all the students will need to succeed in the future study of your subject? Perhaps more importantly, what is the knowledge that you want the students to leave your classrooms with even if they are not going to study this subject any further? How can it bring them power, joy and fulfilment in their lives?

The way that this knowledge needs to be selected is a complex process. Sherrington, writing for Impact, describes knowledge-rich thus: 'Knowledge provides a driving, underpinning philosophy, the grammar of each subject is given high status. Here, 'grammar' relates to the concepts explored by Martin Robinson in *Trivium 21c* (Robinson, 2013) – the knowledge content and traditions within subject disciplines'.[8] In order to maintain the truth of our subjects, there needs to be engagement with our subject communities and the domains in which that knowledge is held and created. This is where your expertise as those who have studied the subject into higher education will be invaluable, and must continue as you must remain up-to-date with the disciplinary practices therein: reading research, reading literature, listening to music, reading criticism, etc. However, it must be understood that, whilst we wish to remain true to the domain of our subject, to recreate this in its entirety in a school context is neither possible nor desirable. What is needed is selection and recontextualisation,[9] so that the diet that our students get is accurate and representative, but manageable and yet enabling: gateway knowledge that pushes them onto harder, stronger knowledge.

What is core knowledge?

Core knowledge is the knowledge we want students to remember long-term; it's the foundational knowledge we hang other knowledge on. Whatever we decide the core knowledge is, it must be returned to and built upon, and taught and assessed in a systematic, repetitive way, to enable students to build a strong schema, or mental model, to underpin their future learning.

What is meant by hinterland?

Hinterland knowledge is particularly seductive, and can often lure us away from the core knowledge because it is usually the most exciting part. The hinterland refers to the extras, the stories, the beautiful details – putting flesh on the bones of the core knowledge. Just like with core knowledge, we need to decide what hinterland knowledge we will teach and why, and what we have to leave out and why. But this process will be even more difficult because the selection is broader! And it is very easy to become distracted by the hinterland and forget that the core knowledge is what we must teach through that hinterland knowledge. So we also need to be clear what hinterland is NOT. Christine Counsell suggests, 'it helps us distinguish between a vital property that makes the curriculum work (the hinterland), and merely 'engaging activities' which distract and make pupils think about the wrong things'. Therefore, your hinterland needs to be a vehicle for the core knowledge that makes the curriculum rich, powerful and cohesive. It should not be based upon teacher preference, what is in the stock cupboard, or 'what we have always done so the PowerPoints just need a bit of tweaking'!

Substantive and disciplinary knowledge

In order to fully understand a knowledge-rich curriculum, there are more key terms you will need to become familiar with. Many criticisms of a knowledge-rich curriculum come from the notion that learning becomes about the rote learning of facts; this is not true. Knowledge is not just facts. There are many different types of knowledge. Substantive knowledge, sometimes also termed declarative knowledge, is hard facts. When we choose which substantive knowledge to teach we need to ask ourselves how it will enhance existing schema, how it will link into the key themes of the curriculum, how rich and beautiful it is and if it fits our curriculum vision. Substantive knowledge is factual knowledge that will remain the same regardless of subject domain; for example: 'London is the capital city of the United Kingdom'. This type of knowledge can indeed be memorised, and in doing so to a state of fluency, or indeed automaticity, students will be provided with a valuable step towards more complex processes, as their working memory is freer to grapple with these larger, more challenging ideas.

However, if we look at disciplinary knowledge, we find a much more complex area that cannot be 'memorised' in such a way (although cognitive science tells us that it will eventually be embedded and stored within the long-term memory). Disciplinary knowledge means how we communicate to students that our subject is a study, a discipline, a tradition, outside of the subject in school; that it moves beyond the curriculum and the tests, and has a value of its own outside of those institutions. For example, an historian and a geographer will treat the idea of London being the capital of the UK in very different ways: an historian would be concerned with the factors which led to the emergence of London as the capital, how London has changed over time, and what caused those changes. Whereas a geographer might focus on its role as a global financial city, population density or how disparities in investment between the north and the south have resulted in north-south divide. These concerns are the disciplinary knowledge of history and geography.

What is procedural knowledge?

For those of you wondering where skills fit into this curriculum, don't worry – they are still important and something that clearly need to be developed. You may hear skills called procedural knowledge, because essentially a skill is another form of knowing – knowing how, for example how to embed quotations into a sentence, how to find grid references on a map, how to create shade with a pencil. A skill is basically knowledge plus practice of that knowledge – so, just like we cannot separate curriculum and pedagogy, we cannot separate knowledge and skills because, as David Didau explains, they are 'two sides of the same coin'.[10] But knowledge must come first, or we will have nothing to practise in order to learn the skill.

What are threshold concepts?

These are difficult, key ideas that allow students to access the next stage of their learning. To write a curriculum as a progression model, we need to identify what these threshold concepts are, when to include them, how to explain them and when and how to return to them to reinforce and develop them. These are likely to be complex and difficult ideas which students will require repeated exposure to in order to be fully understood and to be able to apply them.

Hierarchical and horizontal knowledge

This will differ greatly according to the subject discipline you lead. Basil Bernstein[11] identifies two ways that knowledge in subjects can be structured:

hierarchical and horizontal. Hierarchical knowledge is like a pyramid; it is not possible to learn the second layer of stones without firstly securing those laid at the foundation, and so on to the top. Subjects that are most hierarchical will be the maths and science subjects. Horizontal Knowledge is less dependent on a specific sequence though, which could arguably make these harder to sequence, because there are more options, and rationales, to consider. Subjects within the humanities, and English, are considered to be more horizontal, although they also contain hierarchical elements too.

Ultimate and proximal functions of knowledge

This is about how knowledge manifests. Each section of the curriculum is carefully chosen and is important in serving to prepare students for future content. When we discuss the proximal function of a piece of the curriculum, we mean that it will support the learning that is coming up soon (in close *proximity*) – the learning and content that follows in the coming lessons and weeks. So, this learning makes the next stage of learning possible. For example, learning to identify subjects and verbs in sentences will allow the next stage of learning if that is to learn how to create sentences with more complex syntax: this is its proximal function.

The ultimate function, however, is about enduring learning – its long-term purpose in developing a deep and conceptual understanding of the subject domain. For example, learning to identify subjects and verbs in sentences will allow the students to eventually manipulate language to achieve different effects, as well as recognise the ways that other writers do this themselves, which is part of the construct of English; the ultimate function of this knowledge is that they become part of the subject discipline and even creators of knowledge within it; none of which would be possible without this learning.

How should the curriculum be sequenced?

When we are creating a curriculum sequence, we should be able to see vertical links: concepts that will be revisited repeatedly with your subject as students progress through the school years. In subjects that are more hierarchical, such as maths, the sequencing is particularly crucial, as students' ability to progress relies so much on a sufficient mastery of the procedural knowledge from earlier in the curriculum.

Writing in Impact, Sherrington highlights the importance of sequencing within a knowledge-rich curriculum, explaining that mapping of this knowledge should be done 'deliberately and coherently',[12] with consideration to both the vertical (how knowledge fits with what will be learned later) and horizontal (how knowledge fits with what is being learned concurrently across the curriculum) with the aim of creating 'the optimum knowledge sequence for building secure schema'.[13]

However, Sherrington also highlights the importance of pedagogy, experiences and values within the structuring of this curriculum: 'Attention is also given to known misconceptions, and there is an understanding of the instructional tools needed to move students from novice to expert in various subject domains....A knowledge-rich curriculum is packed with experiences and is driven by a strong set of values about what matters'.[14]

The EEF's research agrees on both the importance of selecting and ordering our knowledge-rich curricula, recognising that a 'common thread, which is certainly to be welcomed, is an emphasis on sequencing. In short, a successful knowledge-rich curriculum should be designed to help pupils remember what they have been taught'.[15] This coincides with Sherrington who explains that what we teach needs to taught so that it is:

> remembered, not merely encountered: A good knowledge-rich curriculum embraces ideas from cognitive science about memory, forgetting and the power of retrieval practice....This requires approaches to curriculum planning and delivery that build in spaced retrieval practice, formative low-stakes testing and plenty of repeated practice for automaticity and fluency.[16]

What is a mastery approach? Do we want to use it, and why?

This brings us to the teaching approach referred to as a mastery approach; this means moving away from self-contained topics that sit in isolation to each other, and instead looking at the curriculum as being cumulative, where content from previous lessons is recalled and reviewed, and the connections in the curriculum are explicitly used to deepen students' knowledge and understanding. And when you structure a curriculum in this way, it allows formative assessment to be used in the best way: by asking questions and returning to the knowledge until everyone has learned it. As Daisy Christodoulou says,

> The most valuable work you can do to create a mastery curriculum is to structure the lessons so that there are frequent opportunities for you to check if pupils have learnt what you have just taught them, and for pupils to recap, review and consolidate their prior learning.[17]

And, by repeatedly asking those questions, it helps us to distinguish between performance, which is measurable, and actual learning, which is not. Robert Bjork says, 'When you introduce things like variability, spacing... interleaving things to be learned rather than blocking the things to be learned; that appears to slow down the learning process and poses challenges but enhances long term retention and transfer'.[18] For example, by using spaced retrieval in our formative assessment we are ensuring that students are remembering over time (learning), not just recalling what they have just been told (performance). And in a mastery curriculum, content is not deemed to have been mastered until approximately 80% of the knowledge test is achieved.

As for 'do we want to use it'? Our answer would be yes. Recent EEF research[19] has shown that a mastery approach to curriculum design and enactment leads to an additional five months' progress, and has been termed as 'promising' for closing the attainment gap.

What is the 'curriculum as progression model'?

All of this leads us to talk about the curriculum using the phrase that Michael Fordham coined, as a progression model.[20] To explain, what we are saying here is that if we design our curriculum really thoroughly to cover what we consider to be the most important elements of the domain, then it is by testing the students' knowledge of that curriculum that we know if and how they are making progress, as well as the effectiveness of our curriculum and its delivery.

Conclusions on knowledge-rich

Therefore, the knowledge-rich approach means taking the most important knowledge you want your students to learn, and ordering it in a way that enables links to be formed and understanding to deepen. Alex Quigley notes its importance, writing: 'By attending to such considerations in our curriculum design, we have a much better chance of ensuring that the knowledge our pupils learn is robust'.[21]

To try and summarise the knowledge-rich approach to curriculum, we can do well by returning to Sherrington's Impact piece which uses the following headings to describe it:

- Knowledge provides a driving, underpinning philosophy. The grammar of each subject is given high status

- The knowledge content is specified in detail

- Knowledge is taught to be remembered, not merely encountered

- Knowledge is sequenced and mapped deliberately and coherently[22]

These are useful as they help us to understand the key idea of knowledge-rich as a concept: the core knowledge of your subject as a discipline is the priority for the content of the curriculum; that knowledge is written down in precise detail so there is equity in content coverage and specificity of which knowledge in a unit is powerful; cognitive science is harnessed to ensure students can and do recall that powerful knowledge and the curriculum is structured to be repetitive, spaced and uses low-stakes formative assessment to ensure this; and that the order of the curriculum content is carefully considered, vertically and horizontally, to ensure the knowledge is imparted at the most appropriate and impactful time to develop students' schemata.

Thus, the knowledge-rich approach entails taking the most important knowledge you want your students to learn, and ordering it in a way that enables links to be formed and understanding to deepen. Questioning ourselves on the content of our curriculum – what we should put in, what must be left out, and why, is therefore a fundamental starting point for curriculum development. This is a discussion which must be held within your subject community of experts. Seek differing opinions, challenge biases and try to evaluate the impact of the choices you are making and the messages you are conveying, perhaps implicitly, through these choices.

Curriculum theory top tips

- Knowledge-rich is a hot-topic word in education at the moment, and it's crucial to be clear on what this means to you and your team, so you can be sure you all have the same objective.

- Make sure you understand all the key terms and concepts first and then make sure your team does too so that you are speaking the same language.

- Focus on your subject and its knowledge, in all its different forms.

- Pay very close attention to sequencing this knowledge so that students master it.

Notes

1 Chris Jones, C. (2018). *Curriculum research: our findings - Ofsted blog: schools, early years, further education and skills.* [online] Educationinspection.blog.gov.uk. Available at: https://educationinspection.blog.gov.uk/2018/09/18/curriculum-research-our-findings/ [Accessed 27 March 2021].
2 Fordham, M. (2020). *What did I mean by 'the curriculum is the progression model'?*. [online] Clio et cetera. Available at: https://clioetcetera.com/2020/02/08/what-did-i-mean-by-the-curriculum-is-the-progression-model/ [Accessed 16 April 2021].
3 Ibid.
4 Ibid.
5 Hirsch, E. D., Kett, J. F., & Trefil, J. (1988). *Cultural literacy: what every American needs to know.* New York, Vintage Books.
6 Quigley, A. (2019). *EEF Blog: What do we mean by 'knowledge rich' anyway?* | *News.* [online] Available at: https://educationendowmentfoundation.org.uk/news/eef-blog-what-do-we-mean-by-knowledge-rich-anyway/ [Accessed 19 March 2021].
7 Young, M. (2020). 'From Powerful Knowledge to the Powers of Knowledge', in Sealy, C. (ed.) *The ResearcEd Guide to the Curriculum.* Melton: John Catt, pp 19–21.
8 Sherrington, T. (2018). *What is a 'knowledge-rich' curriculum?* | *impact.chartered.college.* [online] impact.chartered.college. Available at: https://impact.chartered.college/article/what-is-a-knowledge-rich-curriculum/ [Accessed 21 March 2021].

9 Ashbee, R. (2020). 'Why it's so important to understand school subjects - and how we might begin to do so", in Sealy, C. (ed.) *The ResearcEd Guide to the Curriculum*. Melton: John Catt, pp 31–32

10 Didau, D. (2019). *Skill = knowledge + practice*. [online] David Didau. Available at: https://learningspy.co.uk/learning/you-cant-teach-skills/ [Accessed 27 June 2021].

11 Bernstein, B. (1999). "Vertical and horizontal discourse: An essay." *British Journal of Sociology Education*, 20(2), pp 157–173.

12 Sherrington, T. (2018). *What is a 'knowledge-rich' curriculum? | impact.chartered.college*. [online] impact.chartered.college. Available at: https://impact.chartered.college/article/what-is-a-knowledge-rich-curriculum/ [Accessed 21 March 2021].

13 Ibid.

14 Ibid.

15 Quigley, A. (2019). *EEF Blog: What do we mean by 'knowledge rich' anyway? | News*. [online] Available at: https://educationendowmentfoundation.org.uk/news/eef-blog-what-do-we-mean-by-knowledge-rich-anyway/ [Accessed 19 March 2021].

16 Sherrington, T. (2018). *What is a 'knowledge-rich' curriculum? | impact.chartered.college*. [online] impact.chartered.college. Available at: https://impact.chartered.college/article/what-is-a-knowledge-rich-curriculum/ [Accessed 21 March 2021].

17 Christodoulou, D. (2019). *What is Mastery? The good, the bad, the ugly - Daisy Christodoulou*. [online] Daisy Christodoulou. Available at: https://daisychristodoulou.com/2019/05/what-is-mastery-the-good-the-bad-the-ugly/ [Accessed 27 August 2021].

18 Soderstrom, N. C. and Bjork, R. A. (2015). Learning versus performance: An integrative review. *Perspectives on Psychological Science*, 10(2), pp 176–199.

19 Education Endowment Foundation, 2018. *Mastery learning | Toolkit Strand*. [online] Available at: https://educationendowmentfoundation.org.uk/evidence-summaries/teaching-learning-toolkit/mastery-learning/ [Accessed 18 April 2021].

20 Fordham, M. (2017). *The curriculum as progression model*. [online] Clio et cetera. Available at: https://clioetcetera.com/2017/03/04/the-curriculum-as-progression-model/ [Accessed 17 April 2021].

21 Quigley, A. (2019). *EEF Blog: What do we mean by 'knowledge rich' anyway? | News*. [online] Available at: https://educationendowmentfoundation.org.uk/news/eef-blog-what-do-we-mean-by-knowledge-rich-anyway/ [Accessed 19 March 2021].

22 Sherrington, T. (2018). *What is a 'knowledge-rich' curriculum? | impact.chartered.college*. [online] impact.chartered.college. Available at: https://impact.chartered.college/article/what-is-a-knowledge-rich-curriculum/ [Accessed 21 March 2021].

Bibliography

Ashbee, R. (2020). "Why it's so important to understand school subjects – and how we might begin to do so", in Sealy, C. (ed.) *The ResearcEd Guide to the Curriculum*. Melton: John Catt, pp. 31–32.

Bernstein, B. (1999). "Vertical and horizontal discourse: An essay." *British Journal of Sociology Education, 20*(2), pp 157–173.

Christodoulou, D. (2019). *What is Mastery? The good, the bad, the ugly - Daisy Christodoulou*. [online] Daisy Christodoulou. Available at: https://daisychristodoulou.com/2019/05/what-is-mastery-the-good-the-bad-the-ugly/ [Accessed 27 August 2021].

Chris Jones, C. (2018). *Curriculum research: our findings - Ofsted blog: schools, early years, further education and skills*. [online] Educationinspection.blog.gov.uk. Available at:

https://educationinspection.blog.gov.uk/2018/09/18/curriculum-research-our-findings/ [Accessed 27 March 2021].

Didau, D. (2019). *Skill = knowledge + practice.* [online] David Didau. Available at: https://learningspy.co.uk/learning/you-cant-teach-skills/ [Accessed 27 June 2021].

Education Endowment Foundation, 2018. *Mastery learning | Toolkit Strand.* [online] Available at: https://educationendowmentfoundation.org.uk/evidence-summaries/teaching-learning-toolkit/mastery-learning/ [Accessed 18 April 2021].

Fordham, M. (2017). *The curriculum as progression model.* [online] Clio et cetera. Available at: https://clioetcetera.com/2017/03/04/the-curriculum-as-progression-model/ [Accessed 17 April 2021].

Fordham, M. (2020). *What did I mean by 'the curriculum is the progression model'?.* [online] Clio et cetera. Available at: https://clioetcetera.com/2020/02/08/what-did-i-mean-by-the-curriculum-is-the-progression-model/ [Accessed 16 April 2021].

Hirsch, E. D., Kett, J. F., & Trefil, J. (1988). *Cultural Literacy: What Every American Needs to Know.* New York: Vintage Books.

Quigley, A. (2019). *EEF Blog: What do we mean by 'knowledge rich' anyway? | News.* [online] Available at: https://educationendowmentfoundation.org.uk/news/eef-blog-what-do-we-mean-by-knowledge-rich-anyway/ [Accessed 19 March 2021].

Robinson, M. (2013). *Trivium 21c: Preparing Young People for the Future with Lessons From the Past.* Crown House Publishing.

Robinson, M. (2015). *Trivium 21c.* UK: Independent Thinking Press.

Sherrington, T. (2018). *What is a 'knowledge-rich' curriculum? | impact.chartered.college.* [online] impact.chartered.college. Available at: https://impact.chartered.college/article/what-is-a-knowledge-rich-curriculum/ [Accessed 21 March 2021].

Soderstrom, N.C. and Bjork, R.A. (2015). Learning versus performance: An integrative review. *Perspectives on Psychological Science*, *10*(2), pp. 176–199.

Young, M. (2020). "From Powerful Knowledge to the Powers of Knowledge", in Sealy, C. (ed.) *The ResearcEd Guide to the Curriculum.* Melton: John Catt, pp. 19–21.

5 Curriculum development: the practicalities

As we have said in the previous chapter, creating a new curriculum is an exciting and rewarding task, but it can also be daunting. As a middle leader, you might not have been asked to do this before, or you might have had a part in it but not led on it, so this chapter will look at some of the ways to navigate through this process. Before you can begin to develop the specifics, the groundwork needs to be right to ensure that your work is being developed with the support of the school and will flourish on fertile, academic ground.

What do the conditions need to be for curriculum development to be successful?

Your school needs to be interested in curriculum development to give you and your team (remember, you can't do it alone!) time for CPD, discussion and collaboration; SLT must be prepared to prioritise subject-specific conversations and make space, literally and figuratively, for curriculum to be prioritised; collaborative working must be a culture in the school, with people working as a team to share their ideas and best practice; upskilling through CPD should be the way of doing things – there needs to be a culture of and appetite for subject-specific CPD, and time given over to this to show that it's a priority, not just an empty phrase.

As well as knowing about their subject, teachers will benefit from knowing the principles of effective curriculum design (see the last chapter for detail on this): What do we mean by core, hinterland, disciplinary, substantive, procedural knowledge, ultimate and proximate functions, and threshold concepts, etc.? Does everyone understand the concept of the curriculum as a progression model? Does everyone understand what is meant by a knowledge-rich curriculum? Or a mastery approach? What barriers are there to effective curriculum collaboration, development and implementation? What amazing curriculum is already out there that you can learn from? Before you can begin your work, these are the issues which

DOI: 10.4324/9781003160557-6

need to be addressed at a whole-school as well as department level, and should be the subject of conversations between you and your line manager.

How to audit your current curriculum provision

You might want to begin by thinking about why you are considering changing: has the curriculum been the same for the last ten years? Is it too easy, or too challenging? Have your feeder schools at KS2 had an overhaul which now means there is too much overlap? Are there gaps in students' knowledge at KS4 or KS5 which should be addressed at KS3? Identifying the issues with the current provision will help to steer the direction of the new curriculum.

Ascertaining stakeholder views on the current curriculum is important, too. Surveying teachers, undertaking student voice, gaining parents/carers perspectives will give you useful insights as to how the curriculum is perceived as well as what is working or otherwise. Research other curriculum models by asking for examples on Twitter or looking at blogs, and reading subject-specific books on curriculum design, so you can see what others have put together and the thought processes behind their choices.

Working as a team

If you create a curriculum on your own, what buy-in will there be from your team and those delivering the content? Probably very little. Unless you are a department of one it's really important to show how much you value the expertise of the others in your team by harnessing their knowledge and working together to create something amazing for your school. We appreciate that sometimes, in a stressful and busy school environment, it can feel easier simply to do things yourself, but that means you are missing out on valuable opportunities to develop your team's knowledge of curriculum development, their confidence in and understanding of the new curriculum product, and the chances are that a curriculum made by just one person won't be as rich and effective as one made by many experts. After all, how many of us really know all there is to know about our subjects? Or have the time or energy to do the research necessary to become an expert in every area? Very few of us.

The logistics of how to collaborate should also be considered. What time needs to be set aside e.g. department meetings, CPD slots, etc? Who can you buddy up together? You might want to start by finding out what expertise there is in terms of degree specialisms, master's degrees and outside interests.

Make clear and discuss with your team the timescales and review process you will include, and most importantly ensure that they know that curriculum is an iterative process: it won't be perfect the first time (or ever!) but that by working together the whole will be greater than the sum of its parts.

Another really important point to consider is that people often find change stressful, so ensure you give your team time to think about and act upon changes; telling your department the penultimate week of the summer term that you've decided to change Y7 Autumn 1 is not fair or helpful – it's likely people will be stressed over their holidays, or work to try and put something together quickly and ineffectively. Changing the curriculum should be considered and measured with plenty of notice given so that people don't panic. Remember, being an ethical leader means having reasonable timescales, considering workload and seeking others' opinions.

Costings

Before you get too far into the process, the money needs considering and discussing with SLT and/or finance. How expensive is this going to be? What budget have you got? Work out some rough costings and check them with finance and/or your line manager. Remember to consider CPD costs for new topics, textbooks, booklet production, photocopying and even the cost of cover for curriculum development days. The more you plan for in advance the happier budget holders will be – and the more realistic your planning can be.

Curriculum documentation

Building a curriculum means paperwork. That's because you need to ensure that what is in your head in terms of content and sequencing, as well as the vision and rationale for the curriculum, is clear to people who have not been involved in the process: external visitors, SLT, new staff – you are future-proofing your curriculum so it's useful to all who need or want to see it and use it.

The following are some documents we would suggest are crucial as a backbone to the planning process.

Long-term plans and medium-term plans

There are no 'set' proformas (unless there are some your school or Trust want you to use) so deciding this at the outset will avoid people working to differing goals. Be clear on what you want them to look like and the content for these. A starting point might be to agree the formats with your planning team, and then tweak them as necessary as you go along.

Knowledge intent

In our opinion, these are the most important documents of the curriculum planning process, because everything else hangs from these.

The most straightforward format we have experienced looks something like this, with one for each unit:

	Know: what the students should have working knowledge of	Remember: what students should remember in the longer-term
Big question		
Disciplinary knowledge		
Procedural knowledge		
Tier 2 vocabulary		
Tier 3 vocabulary		

These can of course be adapted to suit the nature of the subject or topic. What is important is that they are a distillation of the main content for each unit, and can be used to ensure an equity of experience for all students. As long as the content from the Knowledge Intents is taught to all students then you know that even with differing approaches to delivery, each student has been given equal access to the knowledge you and your team have decided is the most powerful for each unit.

The Remember column is also then useful for your assessment preparation, as it is this knowledge which will form the bulk of your low-stakes formative assessments, such as recall do now tasks, as well as the summative and synoptic summative assessments throughout the key stage and beyond.

Knowledge Organisers can be really useful in summarising the core knowledge of a unit: If, and it's a big if, KOs are designed collaboratively, and contain only the core knowledge of the topic, and are presented in a consistent way to reduce cognitive load (and by that we mean the amount of working memory students are using – working memory is limited and can only hold a few things as once – maybe as few as four things – before overloading, whereas long-term memory is possibly unlimited), they can be a brilliant assessment resource. They are ideal for use as self-quizzing or testing, so they can take control and prioritise their future learning, and they help students develop independent study habits. You ask students to fill in blank or partially blank KOs as a form of retrieval practise, before using the original to check, and then you can look for common gaps or errors across the class and act accordingly. Starting with the core knowledge contained on the KOs, you can ask why and how questions of the students, for example, how does the theme of sleep link to the theme of corruption in Macbeth?, thus encouraging them to form connections and use the knowledge in different ways. You might decide in your team that you want to use KOs for these reasons, and if so using the Knowledge Intent documents to form their content is a useful idea for ensuring they are streamlined and fit for purpose.

Trackers

Tracking when you introduce concepts and vocabulary, vocabulary definitions and examples, and when to revisit them and deepen them, is important to ensure that key vocabulary has been explicitly taught, and that cognitive overload is avoided by all teachers using the same definitions. Tracking these can also ensure that elaborating on or deepening knowledge of vocabulary, for example with more sophisticated or intangible examples, or giving alternative definitions as relevant, can be handled in a deliberate way so as not to overload and confuse students.

Trackers for formative assessment, e.g. fortnightly quizzes, can be invaluable in terms of ensuring you are interrupting students' forgetting of powerful knowledge, especially that from the 'Remember' column of the knowledge intent document, as well as enabling teachers and departments to see patterns in quizzing data. This will help you more effectively evaluate the success of the curriculum content and delivery; if all students got questions 2 and 4 wrong then there is something amiss in the curriculum's delivery of that knowledge. If just my class got question 3 wrong then I need to re-teach that concept and teach it differently next time around. Using the tracker I can see which class nailed question 3, and ask their teacher how they delivered that knowledge, thus more effectively sharing good practice.

When you are ready to begin, where to actually start?

What is your vision?

This should be in line with the school's vision, but also subject-specific. If the school's vision is 'excellence for all', for example, ask yourself 'what does this look like for my subject?' A vision is more than just words for display: it must be something which is lived and enacted through the curriculum, and must inform your choices around that curriculum. A vision needs to be more than just a tick-box exercise, but something which is discussed and produced collaboratively so everyone feels ownership of and understanding of it – otherwise, it'll just be bubble writing on a display.

When you've established your vision, think about and then discuss the following with your team.

How do we go about designing a curriculum as a progression model?

As discussed above, we need to ask ourselves: What powerful knowledge are we going to teach? What do students already know, from primary school, from their last school year, from social culture, from home and their own experiences? How do we build on this and go beyond it? Bernstein says that powerful knowledge allows us to, 'think the unthinkable',[1] so what is that powerful knowledge in your subject? Is it World War I? Is it the Industrial Revolution? Is it sentence structure, or rhetoric? And within those broad topics, which elements do we delve deeper into, which do we gloss over, and which do we leave out all together? With a finite amount of time we must carefully select when goes in, and what is left out, and understand and be able to articulate and review the rationale behind those choices.

As the curriculum leader, it may be a good idea to create this framework overview first of all yourself – a model that can be used to show your vision and help your team to understand the journey that you envision. The level of specificity required may well be underestimated as this is another characteristic of a knowledge-rich curriculum that may be different to previous expectations. Sherrington, in his Impact piece, describes, *The knowledge content is specified in detail: Units of work are supported by statements that detail the knowledge to be learned – something that can be written down.... This runs through every phase of school: units of work are not defined by headings but by details.*[2] You must then be ready for them to question, dismantle, and rebuild your framework when you present it to them for feedback, which should be your next move. After gathering this feedback, rework the overview taking what makes sense, but also providing rationale for what you have not acted upon; this will make your team see, and feel, that you have considered their input rather than just dismissing it automatically.

What core knowledge do we want to teach, and why?

Having set out and agreed upon your framework, for now (as this will no doubt change several times as you move through the process), then it's time to start on the more detailed planning of the units within this. Again, do not underestimate the amount of time that will be required, and do not rush this process. Consider what level of detail you want this to be done in, and the format of the documents and resources that will be used. Again, this is a discussion to have with your team, several of whom may have useful examples which can be used or combined to create a masterpiece. You should also consider how you can make the cohesion of your units most effective and efficient: a single page document which details all of the core knowledge you want your students to remember from that unit moving forwards will be a valuable reference point to return to when planning the future units, planning in retrieval practice, as well as for ensuring that the unit in hand achieves its aims.

Having outlined the core knowledge that you want to be included in that unit as a group, now may be a good time to empower your team members by asking them to work on individual units. This is a wonderful place to explore the specialisms and interests of your department: which teacher or pair of teachers have the best knowledge of that area of your subject? Dividing up the responsibility and playing to the strengths of the team will create a sense of ownership and make everyone feel their expertise is appreciated and valued, as well as meaning that you get the benefit of the pool of knowledge you have at your disposal.

Start at the beginning with your first unit in Year 7. Depending on the experience within your department, and their grasp of your endeavour, you may want to take on this unit yourself so that you can model what you would like a unit to look like. This could save members of the department a lot of time, and perhaps resentment, if they slave for a long time over something that is ultimately not fit for the purpose you had in mind. Create your reference document containing the knowledge you wish to include, and then divide this up over the unit. Create a medium-term plan which shows what knowledge is taught where. Then create the resources you would like to be used; this could be a booklet that encompasses the unit, or lesson PowerPoints. Perhaps you wish to be highly prescriptive about particular elements of the resources, and this can be a positive thing, especially when, inevitably, there comes a time when non-specialists and cover teachers deliver your curriculum, because a highly prescriptive option sets out a minimum guarantee for the students in each class. However, be mindful of over-prescription, and when presenting your work to your team, you should again listen to and act on their feedback, and could make it clear that, so long as the knowledge that is outlined on the medium-term plan is learned, then flexibility is welcomed and encouraged so that teachers have the autonomy to adapt to suit their own classes.

Once curriculum planning is underway in this manner, then you may be tempted to look towards a time when this will be a job ticked off. However, as Howard and Hill tell us in *Symbiosis*, 'curriculum work is never finished, but the value is to be found in the process and not in a non-existent end-point' therefore, your hope, and expectation, should be that these conversations will continue past this initial phase of writing new units for your new curriculum. There should be continued and planned-in evaluation of your curriculum ongoing as part of your meeting time together, making up a repeated section on your department meeting schedule.

What substantive knowledge will we focus on?

We know that substantive knowledge is the hard facts of the domain, and that when we choose which substantive knowledge to teach, we need to ask ourselves how it will enhance existing schema, how it will link into the key themes of the curriculum, how rich and beautiful it is, and if it fits our curriculum vision.

Make a list of the substantive knowledge of your subject; which of this has been taught at KS2; which needs revising or deepening; which is suitable for KS4 or 5 study; which is crucial for KS3; what is the best order to teach it in and why? Review the list with your curriculum development team to ensure you haven't missed out something vital, and to agree on the sequencing and rationale.

What hinterland are we going to explore?

We know that the hinterland is the flesh on the bones of the curriculum, the vehicle through which we teach and through which students remember the powerful knowledge we are imparting; the stories we use to bring the knowledge to life. But this means that it can be easy to get it wrong. For example, when Lyndsay was teaching the poem 'My Last Duchess' to her GCSE classes, she used to 'teach' (using the term loosely), two lessons where the students put the Duke and Duchess on trial. We had the two characters, the judge, two lawyers and the rest of the class were the jury. We all had a ball. And the two students playing the Duke and Duchess knew their characters quite well, but the rest of the class had a jolly. They always remembered those lessons and talked about them, but they didn't remember the content of the poem. She would have been much better off, and so would her students, had she explicitly taught them about the role of women and the patriarchy in the Renaissance, and Browning's place as a Victorian poet and how he might have been influenced by the preceding Romantic poets such as Wordsworth and Coleridge – that would have been worthwhile hinterland knowledge, not who acted as a judge for two lessons. We want Hinterland knowledge to pique the curiosity and intellect of our subject, foster a passion for it because of the power and beauty of the knowledge we are imparting.

What are the key threshold concepts and disciplinary knowledge we need students to master?

The next area we need to think about is threshold concepts. What are the difficult ideas we need to teach – those that, until mastered, students cannot move beyond a certain point? What order do these need to be introduced in? When and how often do these need to be revisited – because these are difficult they will need repeating and revising.

In terms of the disciplinary knowledge, we must ask ourselves how we address this in our teaching, so we are sensitive to the wider importance of the subject, and so we are preparing students for potential further study? Again, review the list with your curriculum development team to ensure you haven't missed out something vital, and to agree on the sequencing and rationale.

What procedural knowledge will we include?

Procedural knowledge is another key area we need to think carefully about: and when we're talking about procedural knowledge we mean how we go about implementing, or teaching the implementation of, certain knowledge. When designing a curriculum, we need to be deliberately consistent in our teaching of procedural knowledge in order to reduce the impact of learning new methods on students' working memory. If all teachers use the same terminology, procedures, systems, acronyms, etc, we reduce students' extraneous cognitive load, give a sense of cohesion and commonality to our curriculum as well as ensuring equity of experience. So the key decisions to be made are what procedural knowledge do we need to prioritise and how do we teach it in a consistent way.

How will the learning be sequenced?

This brings us nicely on to the next element we need to carefully consider; the sequencing of the curriculum. To make the most of the powerful knowledge we are teaching, we need to ensure it is sequenced in a cohesive way, so that one unit connects to another meaningfully, in a way that will expand students' schema – so even though the content will be different, we are still revisiting and building on the concepts of the discipline. This allows students to use that prior knowledge to inform the next steps of their learning.

What about cross-curricular links?

Another facet of effective curriculum design is making sensitive and appropriate interdisciplinary links with other subjects. If you are in the position where there is a whole-school review of curriculum then this could be an invaluable opportunity to look at links between subjects, and possibilities for careful connections to be made across the breadth of the school's curricula. Concepts, vocabulary and procedural knowledge, amongst others, can be mapped across and between different subjects' curricula, with areas of commonality identified.

Robin Fogerty's research in this area provides a good starting point for identifying where your school is, from a fragmented model, where all subjects are separate and distinct, and cross-curricular connections are implicit or accidental, or the sequenced model, where teaching of themes or eras are consciously arranged simultaneously or concurrently so that links between subjects can be explicitly drawn, and so on. Fogerty suggests different types of curriculum integration such as the webbed curriculum, which uses themes to draw together similar concepts and topics cross-curricularly, or an integrated model, where overlapping concepts are used in a disciplinary way, for example in a whole-school literacy focus on writing.[3]

These models all have different pros and cons, but the benefit of making links, if done well, is that students should be able to draw upon their knowledge from one area of the broader curriculum to expand and further embed and synthesise their knowledge in another subject. It's a good idea to decide how much integration you want to aim for, using Fogerty's research to help you understand the varying levels of links which can be made. If it is too ambitious or unachievable to look across a five-year curriculum, then starting with one unit as a trial is a good place to start.

For this work to be done effectively, time needs to be allowed for teacher collaboration, conversations between subject experts, and this must be facilitated at whole-school level. As a middle-leader your advocating of this approach, or your leading of small-scale trialling to prove effectiveness, could be very influential in steering this as a whole-school initiative.

How is it going to be assessed?

It may be that you have an assessment system in your school that shapes how you feedback, mark and assess, but as a middle leader you have a role in influencing the future of those policies and systems, as well as adapting them to be sensitive to the context of your subject. Discuss assessment with your team, and decide what you want your formative and summative assessments to look like. How will you ensure you are assessing students' expanding domain knowledge? How is procedural knowledge assessed? If and how you might capture formative assessment feedback and how to act on it. The chapter on Assessment in this book will give you more detail on the pros and cons of different approaches to all these issues.

Christine Counsell suggests that *The curriculum itself is the progression model. Its mastery is progress....When it comes to progress, the burden of proof is on the curriculum...it is not just a setting in which to practise skills; it is a curricular property with an agency all of its own.*[4] This means that we must measure students' progress through their knowledge and understanding of the curriculum content – and not just for exams or data, but for the intrinsic, social, power and value that knowledge holds in and of itself.

Evaluating the curriculum

How do we measure whether the new curriculum has worked? We might use test results, formative and summative assessments, student voice, teachers' perspectives, parents/carers feedback, book-looks, KS4 or 5 results ... the list goes on. Christine Counsell suggests the following: *A curriculum exists to change the pupil, to give the pupil new power. One acid test for a curriculum is whether it enables even lower-attaining or disadvantaged pupils to clamber into the discourse and practices of educated people, so that they gain the powers of the powerful.*[5]

This way of considering the lower-prior-attaining students' progress through the curriculum as a benchmark for its success is powerful; by really interrogating this as a measure of success we hold ourselves to account and insist on the highest standards for ourselves and all of our students.

Conclusion

Creating a curriculum is important, exciting and hard work. As a middle leader, you will be the linchpin of the project, shaping the thinking and direction of the knowledge and content, turning the school vision for education into specific content for your subjects and students, and building something beautiful and powerful for you and your team to experience with your students. Asking yourselves the questions in this chapter is the start of the journey, because the curriculum is never finished. Make lists and sequence them: be specific and granular in the knowledge you will teach and in what order. That is the underpinning of the curriculum and will form the structure of your long-term planning.

Top tips for leading curriculum development

- Work as a team: you can't do it alone, and why would you want to? The more ideas and expertise the better. Harness the specialities in your team and utilise their knowledge.

- Establish your vision at the start: this will underpin the decisions you make and will help when there is a difference of opinion about content.

- Talk with SLT: It's important they know the scope and direction of your ideas, so they can support you with time, resources and challenge. Curriculum work is hard and you will need to have their support and understanding.

- Make lists and sequence them: be specific and granular in the knowledge you will teach and in what order. That is the underpinning of the curriculum and will form the structure of your long-term planning.

- Build in evaluation: you probably won't get it right the first time, and curriculum work is never finished. Build in reflection points, and don't be disheartened if a unit doesn't work as you envisaged the first time through.

Notes

1 Bernstein, Basil. (1996). Pedagogy, Symbolic Control and Identity: Theory, Research, Critique. London: Taylor & Francis.
2 Sherrington, T. (2018). 'What is a 'Knowledge-Rich' Curriculum?', Impact, Chartered College of Teaching, https://impact.chartered.college/wp-content/uploads/2018/03/Sherrington-Article.pdf
3 Fogarty, R. (1991). Ten ways to integrate curriculum. *Educational leadership*, *49*(2), pp. 61–65.
4 Counsell, C. (April 2018). 'Senior Curriculum Leadership 1: The indirect manifestation of knowledge: (B) final performance as deceiver and guide', The Dignity of the Thing, https://thedignityofthethingblog.wordpress.com/author/christinecounsell/
5 Counsell, C. (April 2018). 'Senior Curriculum Leadership 1: The indirect manifestation of knowledge: (B) final performance as deceiver and guide', The Dignity of the Thing, https://thedignityofthethingblog.wordpress.com/author/christinecounsell/

Bibliography

Bernstein, Basil. (1996). *Pedagogy, Symbolic Control and Identity: Theory, Research, Critique*. London: Taylor & Francis.

Counsell, C. (April 2018). "Senior Curriculum Leadership 1: The indirect manifestation of knowledge: (B) final performance as deceiver and guide." *The Dignity of the Thing*, https://thedignityofthethingblog.wordpress.com/author/christinecounsell/.

Fogarty, R. (1991). Ten ways to integrate curriculum. *Educational Leadership*, *49*(2), pp. 61–65.

Sherrington, T. (2018). "What is a 'Knowledge-Rich' Curriculum?", *Impact, Chartered College of Teaching*, https://impact.chartered.college/wp-content/uploads/2018/03/Sherrington-Article.pdf.

6 | Teaching and learning

Everything else that we are doing as teachers and leaders will mean very little if learning is not actualised effectively within our classrooms: this is where it matters, where the fruits of the thinking, planning, discussing, revising, meeting, networking, recruiting will come to grow and flourish. And that is why the importance of our pedagogy cannot be overstated.

As a middle leader, as ever, there is more than one way that you can get it wrong in this crucial area. The first being how well-informed you are in educational research, and ensuring that your team is employing what evidence shows is the most effective way for students to learn. If you are lucky, your senior leadership team may be excellent in feeding this down to you and your team, and implementing evidence-informed initiatives to develop teaching and learning across the school in line with up-to-date research; however, this is not always the case, and this should not stop you from ensuring that your department is the trailblazer, providing exemplary practice to share with others. Also, there are always aspects of pedagogy that are subject-dependent, and you should be ensuring that you are selective in your techniques to remain true to this. There are, however, some key recommendations which will be effective across the board in helping your students to learn knowledge and skills, and we hope to share some of that motivational knowledge with you in this chapter.

Case Study: Deb Rothwell, English Teacher

It's not that long ago that I was quite disillusioned about teaching. I had given up my Head of Department role, dropped down to just two days of teaching, and I think all this was largely because teaching English at that time, in that context, felt like training students for GCSE exams, by constantly getting them to write things that were like GCSE exam responses. How dull is that? The excitement was supposed to be found in text choices (which I often found unchallenging, but that didn't seem to matter so long as you could get them to write a Paper 1 Question 2 response about a character description from 'Holes'), or from including 'engaging' activities in lessons like going and finding things around the room. But this wasn't why I liked English. And it wasn't why I wanted my students to like English. And, moreover, it didn't really

DOI: 10.4324/9781003160557-7

seem to make a lot of difference to their progress: those who did well were the ones who I knew would do well, and those who didn't were sadly the expected ones too – and this was largely based on their backgrounds and prior attainment. What difference was I actually making? I felt impotent.

Then, I was introduced to cognitive science, and it changed everything. Suddenly, I had the knowledge of what happens when learning takes place, why it's so important to structure our planning using this knowledge, and how to use this knowledge to make a difference in my classroom: to find the excitement in the actual subject I went into teaching because of my love for, and to ignite my students' excitement for that subject too. I was moved from impotence to impetus.

Cognitive psychology

For some of you, this may be an introduction to some of these concepts and ideas; for others, this will be revision of theories you have encountered before, but, we're sure that knowing about how cognitive science works, you will know how valuable that it is in itself! So, we will now take you through: what cognitive science is with a focus on working memory, long-term memory, and schemata; why understanding cognitive science is important for us as teachers; and how we can use cognitive science to make ourselves and our teams better teachers, because that is what we are all constantly striving to be.

The foundation of cognitive science is memory. And this is a complex area: we could spend many hours discussing the research findings about memory, but the fundamental components we must understand as teachers are: working memory and long-term memory. Working memory is where thinking happens. When we ask our students a question about the text we are reading in our lesson, and they get that vaguely perplexed look on their face, it's because they are grappling with information in their working memory. And that is difficult, because working memory is limited: it is like a shoe box. Firstly, it is limited in terms of duration: if information is not repeated after 18–30 seconds then it can be forgotten forever. Secondly, it is limited in terms of capacity: although disputed, the number of items that we can hold in our working memory ranges from around four to seven chunks of information.[1] And, as far as current research tells us, there is no way to increase this.

Long-term memory is very different, however. Imagine, if you will, a huge reference library where you have your own personal librarian who records and stores away information for another time. As opposed to working memory, we do not know the limitations of long-term memory.

What is also important is how working memory and long-term memory interact. Because this is essentially how learning is created. Daniel Willingham tells us that 'memory is the residue of thought' and this concept can be transformational to understanding teaching and learning. We need to ensure that the working memory contains the information that we want students to be thinking about, and that they think hard about it, so that they transfer it to their long-term memory. To ensure that this happens, it means that we need to think carefully about how many pieces, or chunks, of information, we are presenting to our students at a time, ensuring that they think hard about them in order to put them into their long-term memory, before moving onto the next chunks. This links to the work of John Sweller on Cognitive Load Theory, which tells us that the instructional methods that we use should avoid overloading the working memory because this will help to maximise learning.[2] These chunks of information will not just live in isolation in the long-term memory though – they will link onto other related chunks, creating schema and understanding this process is at the heart of understanding how to structure our curriculum and our lessons (Figure 6.1).

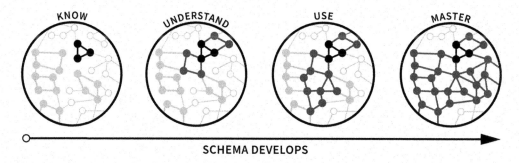

Figure 6.1 Dr Efrat Furst's model of stages of learning in long-term memory store, working memory and strategies to develop[3].

Dr Efrat Furst explains four stages in the learning model: the first, knowing, means that we recognise something that we have seen before. Secondly, understanding involves connecting the new piece of information to something you already know: prior knowledge. Then there is using this understood knowledge in different contexts, creating more connections in the brain. Finally, when this has been used enough times and in enough contexts, mastering occurs – when enough connections have been made so that this knowledge has become part of the brain's schemas: the models in the brain that will act as a platform for new learning so that this process can continue. We need to make sure that this platform is solid so that future learning has strong foundations.[4]

This can be seen in the structure of the introducing any new learning such as in maths where students are introduced to the concept of quadrilaterals as a piece of knowledge, they use this knowledge in subsequent lessons to develop understanding by applying it to further examples, noting similarities and differences, followed by using the rules of quadrilaterals to problem-solve. By repeating this rule in different exercises, and applying it in different contexts and quizzes until they achieve mastery of it: once they have mastered it, they can use it as a platform for new learning about knowledge of different types of shapes, for example, and begin the process of mastering those.

Some of you may be wondering how this all really applies to your subjects. After all, haven't we been told for so long that many of our subjects are skills-based? And weren't we told that teaching itself was 'Outstanding' when it was focused on 'generic learning skills'. Teachers of English certainly were.

Case Study: continued Deb Rothwell Teacher of English

'English at the Crossroads' was published in 2009,[5] telling English teachers that teachers should be using creative, practical approaches, involving students in creating the curriculum, avoiding directing the students too much. Boxer-like, I adopted my 'Ofsted knows best' mantra and did all these sorts of lessons in which I thought were promoting Personal Learning and Thinking skills by asking them to work in groups to create their own newspaper, or designing a costume for a tribute from The Hunger Games, but they didn't know enough to be making any connections that created learning. And they certainly weren't thinking hard enough to create this residue that is memory – the only memory they probably had was whatever gossip they were chatting with their mates about. They certainly enjoyed lots of these types of texts because they were culturally familiar to them, which was also deemed to be a good thing, largely because how we taught was seen as much more important than what we taught.

Thankfully, this has changed. Because it isn't actually possible to separate what we teach (the curriculum) and how we teach it (pedagogy). And what we teach is extremely important. Curriculum time is finite and extremely precious. We don't want to teach our students something that they are familiar with – why teach them something that they already know? We want to teach them something culturally rich – to take them out of their everyday lived experience of the world and show them everything else that is out there in the world and in humanity – because that is what education is! And we want these students to know about 'the best that has been thought and said' in our subject – it is through this that we will build their cultural capital, allowing them wider access to the world.

But doesn't all this putting information into the long-term memory just mean memorising facts? Aren't most, or all, of our subjects skills-based? Well, no – it's much more complicated than that. As discussed further in our chapter on the theory of curriculum development, knowledge is not just facts. There are many different types of knowledge: declarative knowledge, knowing what, for example, Mr Bumble being a corrupt character, or the elements on the periodic table. This is no new concept either as it harks back to Ancient Greece when Aristotle would have termed this episteme.

Another type is procedural knowledge or knowing how, for example how to embed quotations into a sentence or how to use a Bunsen burner in a scientific experiment. For Aristotle, this would be techne. David Didau explains that to learn a skill, we need to have knowledge about the rules that are at the root of that skill, and then to practise it. Without first putting in place the knowledge before practice, we rely on that which our students are bringing with them, and this advantages those who come to us with greater stores of knowledge already in place which is usually those who are not from disadvantaged backgrounds.[6]

And what makes our subjects so wonderful, but also so wonderfully difficult, is that they hold so many different types and areas of knowledge which must interact for one to be successful at them. We are all victims of the curse of the expert, having gone into teaching due to loving our subjects, and probably being pretty good at them. To relate to our case study, think of the expertise involved in creating a literary essay in English, for example. So many stores of knowledge are being drawn on to complete that task: of the text, the various component parts of how to write an essay, themes, motifs, the writer, history, current context, vocabulary, connotations, terminology, quotations, devices, spelling, syntax, paragraphing, handwriting ... we could go on. Each of these things has to be mastered to make this successful. Our primary colleagues will hopefully have planned for mastery of some of the knowledge that is needed to be successful in our subjects, but we need to build upon this prior learning and upon those foundations so that each component takes them closer to having overall mastery of our domain. This is why it is important that we do not ask our students to do too much too soon – they need to practise and master each component part of your subjects and build them up sequentially in order for each to be successful. This relates to our chapter on assessment, and why we should be moving away from the GCSE-lite style assessments from the start of KS3 too – we only need to assess what we have taught, because this is what we need to know about in the mastery in our students' brains, and assessing them on knowledge and skills that we haven't taught them yet is unfair, and inefficient.

Practical application

Finally, we come to what is probably the most important part of this: how do we make this work for us, with our students in our classrooms?

We have probably all felt that disillusionment when the content we worked so hard at teaching a few weeks previously seems to have completely disappeared from our classes' brains. Ebbinghaus's forgetting curve from 1885 shows us that, even though we may be teaching our best teaching and working so hard, only a small amount remains as time goes on – what a depressing thought. However, there is a solution to this: retrieval practice, or harnessing the benefits of 'the testing effect' (Figure 6.2).

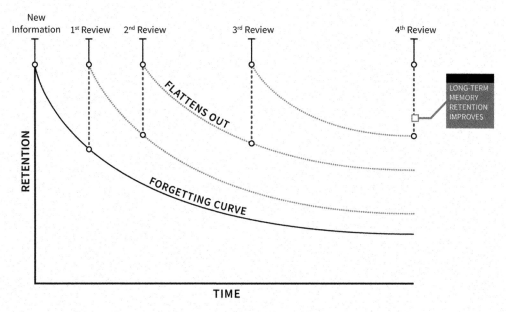

Figure 6.2 Typical Forgetting Curve for Newly Learned Information[7].

As you see, by regularly testing, or retrieving this content, we can make sure that this knowledge doesn't disappear – more and more is retained each time as the connections in the brain get stronger: this is us planning for these strong schema for our students. This is because, as Robert Bjork says, 'Using our memory shapes our memory'.[8]

Retrieval

As explained previously, working memory cannot be increased. We cannot do that for our students. However, we can help to free up some space in that working memory for them so that they have room to grapple with the more complex ideas that are so common in our subjects. We know that learning in any subject is not just the memorisation of facts, because domains are so rich and complex. But facts do matter: to return to the complex task of writing a literary essay, we would need to know who William Shakespeare is, the name of the play, the plot of the play, a quotation, the definitions of vocabulary, in order to write about them with meaning. By retrieving this information enough times so that our students have fluency over this important knowledge, as it is now securely stored in the long-term memory, creating automaticity, we can free up that important working memory space for them to consider the more complex ideas we are aiming for.

Furthermore, we are able to influence the schemata in our students' brains, by using retrieval practice to create the links between their prior and current learning for them. The start of a lesson is an ideal place for retrieval. By using a Do Now[9] activity to start the lesson with retrieval, we can maximise the learning in that lesson. It is wise to use questions to firstly review the learning from the last lesson. Questions can also be framed to use some of the vocabulary previously taught in different ways in order to develop the connections in the students' brains with these older pieces of information. If we want to ensure that the students make connections between the learning that is happening in the current lesson and something they learned about a few weeks previously, we can ensure that we focus a question on that, meaning that every student has that information ready to link onto what they are exposed to today. It is important to build the difficulty within the retrieval by putting in knowledge that will have been encountered even longer ago: perhaps the last year or even prior to this, depending on what they will be putting into use in this lesson; this may be knowledge that has been taught right at the start of their learning, but has been retrieved sequentially throughout the subsequent years. By choosing what we want the students to think about at the start of this lesson, we are helping them to ignite that prior learning that will create the schemata that will in turn become a strong foundation for future learning.

But the start of a lesson is not the only place for retrieval. Another excellent place for retrieval in the classroom is through questioning, and this can be particularly effective during modelling. For example, as we are modelling a paragraph on, perhaps Macbeth for GCSE students, we can be asking targeted questions to recall knowledge about the plot, characters, quotations, etc.

Spacing and interleaving

This particularly links to spacing and interleaving. These are both examples of what are called 'desirable difficulties'[10]: elements that make learning better, because they make the students think more, and as we know, Willingham told us that 'memory is the residue of thought'[11] so more thought will create stronger memory.

Often there is a confusion between performance and learning. We see high performance and think that learning has taken place but actually we are not seeing learning; learning will only take place over time, and we actually need to slow learning down, and make it harder to make it more effective. Bjork and Bjork explain that 'Conditions of learning that make performance improve rapidly often fail to support long-term retention, whereas conditions that create challenges and slow the rate of apparent learning often optimize long-term retention'.[12] Therefore, desirable difficulties are elements that will create this slower, more thoughtful process of learning

These concepts of spacing and interleaving are both very important, but very often confused. What we have been describing here with the examples of retrieval, have been acts of spacing: the act of deliberately leaving a space between practice of content – deliberately letting them forget, but then making them remember just at the right moment.

Interleaving is another of Bjork's desirable difficulties. Very simply, it means switching between ideas whilst you are learning. In terms of planning, this means that, rather than teaching content in one block, we ensure that they are exposed to this 'block' of content spread across the curriculum, perhaps some in term 1, some in term 2 and some in term 3. This is different from spaced retrieval because this is merely recalling the same information; with interleaving, we are continuing the learning, but we have distributed the progression of this learning over the curriculum. Whilst interleaving is being categorised as 'desirable' here, it is worth noting that it is often regarded as working better in some subjects, for example maths wherein there is a lot of research to show its effectiveness, rather than others like humanities where there is not a great deal of evidence to support its positive effects on learning; this is somewhere for middle leaders to use their professional judgement and, again, think about what works best for their own subject domain.

Threshold concepts

Another important aspect of cognitive science to consider is threshold concepts. This is a very important idea to consider, particularly looking at wider curriculum planning.

These so-called 'jewels of the curriculum'[13] are complex, core ideas of the subject that require mastering before it is possible to move to the next level. However, not only will they serve as a gateway, or indeed a 'threshold' to future learning, they can also reconfigure what has been learned before. A bit like when you find out who the murderer is in a drama, and looking back, it sheds a whole new light on everything they did and said.

One of the best explanations of threshold concepts is to be found in Claire Hill and Kat Howard's *Symbiosis*.[14] As well as their transformative and irreversible qualities, and the way they integrate pieces of knowledge to connect them together, they also explain their features as 'Bounded' in that they are 'tightly woven into the discipline of one subject and unlikely to transfer to another'[15] and also 'Troublesome' because their complexity can exceed the learner's level of understanding, and thus our teaching of them needs to be treated with special care, collaboratively working on shared language and explanations'.[16]

The idea of threshold concepts brings us back to our case study:

Case Study: Deb Rothwell continued

Learning about cognitive science was a threshold concept for me: a transformative moment that enabled me to see the bigger picture in the world of education. It has aided development of my schema linking smaller chunked pieces of information in my long-term memory and thus enabled a gateway to develop more complex schemas moving forward. This means that I now have the power to change the way I think about learning, and that means I have the power to change the way students learn about English: by planning for the careful, sequential exposure to knowledge, that is broken into spaced and interleaved chunks, that the students are able to think hard about and master before moving on to the next thing, particularly when it is something as important as a threshold concept.

Practicalities of teaching and learning

Again returning to the concept that 'Memory is the residue of thought',[17] no matter what curriculum area you are leading, you want your students to remember the contents of the curriculum that you have carefully curated; this means that your primary focus in every moment in every lesson should be: what are my students thinking about? Are they all thinking? How hard are they thinking?

Extraneous load

In terms of what your students are thinking about, you want this to be focused on the core content of your curriculum, and this means removing extraneous load: if they are thinking about the funny gif on a presentation slide, or the joke that the teacher digressed to tell them, or the balloon they are popping, are they going to be thinking about the mathematical equation, scientific formula, or poetic technique you want them to remember? By simplifying our pedagogy, and taking away the superfluous elements that we may have been told are necessary to make our subjects engaging, we reveal what is truly engaging, and beautiful: the knowledge at the heart of these subjects that we love and that brought us to teach them.

Participation ratio

Once we have ensured that the students are thinking about the right thing, we want to make sure that there is equity across our classrooms, and that all the students are engaged in thinking: this is termed 'participation ratio' by Doug Lemov in *Teach Like a Champion 2.0,*[18] and we want to keep this high from the moment a lesson begins. Therefore, you will want your team to have a repertoire of techniques that will engage and maintain this, whilst staying true to the curriculum focus. Very often, teachers begin a topic or lesson or learning sequence with discussion by asking for students to contribute by putting their hands up to speak. This does not achieve a high participation ratio, and also means that it is difficult for the teacher to guide the classroom discourse. Some ideas for how to structure this differently are explained by Paul Bambrick-Santoyo in *Leverage Leadership 2.0.*[19] They include having the students all writing before any discussion happens, so that all students have some ideas ready, and the teacher (who monitors this) can select the stronger responses to call upon in the discussion that follows; another option is a Turn and Talk followed by polling the room which means that all of the students have been engaged in a short discussion and therefore there can be no excuses for not having an answer prepared when the teacher cold-calls any student for their ideas. Other techniques to maximise participation ratio include: retrieval practice of substantive knowledge, starting with clear answers that you are confident every learner will know, effective use of cold call with wait time before giving the name of the student you wish to answer, choral response, and mini-whiteboards. For more on these techniques, look to Lemov's *Teach Like a Champion 2.0*[20] for detailed explanations and examples.

Thinking ratio

Professor Robert Coe tells us that, 'Learning happens when people have to think hard'.[21]

If all the learners are engaged in thinking, we then need to develop their thinking ratio,[22] making them gradually think harder and more deeply about this important content. This will mean that lessons need to be carefully structured with an easily retrieved question to build confidence developing towards more challenging spaced retrieval in a Do Now activity, for example, and the development of a string of questioning to stretch, make connections and build to increasingly conceptual ideas during teacher-led discussion.

Maximising time

But how do you encourage and develop the most effective teaching strategies within your team? Firstly, you can make effective use of meeting time; this time is finite and should not be just used for administrative tasks that can often be conducted over email or a well-constructed Microsoft Form or Google document! Use your time together to engage in the things that really matter: curriculum and pedagogy. Depending on the experience of your team, you may need to use this time to introduce these techniques. This should be done at a steady pace, focusing on one at a time. Start with the research, so that your team knows why they are doing it, how effective it will be. Then you need to model what it looks like in the classroom, literally: conduct the meeting in the classroom, with your team as the students in order to start creating mental models for them of what they need to create in their own practice. You can then follow this with some deliberate practice, with each teacher trying out the technique in the same way, and receiving immediate feedback. What would be even better would be if it wasn't you, as the curriculum leader, modelling the technique each time though. Having used some of your leadership time to engage in learning walks of your department, identify those in your team who are strong in that area and ask them to demonstrate and model, with you taking part in the deliberate practice and taking on feedback from the team to exemplify that everyone is learning and developing their practice together constantly: this is collaborative and not a top-down approach. Once a technique has been practised in these controlled conditions, you need to see how it looks 'in the wild', so your next learning walks should focus on how well it is landing in the classroom, and seeing if there are any tweaks that are needed to improve. Once you are happy that this technique is being used at a good standard, you can try to embed a new technique.

Co-planning

Another important part of your departmental time will be looking at planning as a team. After you have honed your units (see the chapters on curriculum development), there is still further work to do as you need to continue to tweak and mould your planning and resourcing for use in the classroom. The best thing to do here is have weekly co-planning sessions. If you are extremely lucky, you will get these timetabled as a department. If not, you may need to be more creative about how you find the time to get your whole department together; it may be use of directed meeting time, or by using some PPA (this is planning time, so your team may understand the value from sharing this planning time together, but tread carefully here), it may be doing co-planning less frequently whilst you work on persuading SLT how valuable it is (inviting them along to some sessions and seeing the resulting lessons, perhaps).

Your co-planning sessions will have two different formats: the first will be when preparing to teach a unit. We would advise that the facilitator of the session (this may be you, or perhaps a second in your department) has a sheet with prepared notes that covers:

- the overall aim of the unit,

- how it links to prior and future learning,

- the core substantive and disciplinary knowledge,

- tier two and three vocabulary,

- challenges and misconceptions that are foreseen,

- how you will know that students have been successful in this unit,

- and what subject knowledge development or other preparation team members might need to do before teaching the unit.

Whilst you will have prepared notes on all of these areas, the other members of the team should have blank copies with these headings so that you can lead them in making their own notes and pooling ideas. It will be important to have the full overview of the unit so that the team can see the full structure of the unit, as well as any documents like knowledge intents, key texts and background reading that is essential. Every member of the team should leave this co-planning session with a very clear and shared understanding of what they are aiming to achieve in teaching this unit, but moreover why they are teaching it, and also the specific two or three ways they are going to prepare to do it really well.

Following on from this, you can use subsequent sessions to look more closely at how the individual lessons are taught. Clearly, you are not going to have time to co-plan every single lesson together, so be selective and choose the ones that you think are going to be the most challenging for your team, or are the most representative of the lesson style, meaning that it will be easily replicated during personal planning. In this lesson-focused session, you can follow a similar format to the preparing to teach one, but your preparation notes will focus on:

- the overall aim of the lesson,

- how it links to prior and future learning,

- the core substantive and disciplinary knowledge,

- tier two and three vocabulary,

- specific misconceptions that may arise and how they will be dealt with,

- challenging content and how this will be scaffolded,

- ways that teachers can provide additional challenge whilst remaining faithful to the curriculum being the progression model,

- how you will know that students have been successful in this lesson,

- and any specific preparation team members might need to do before teaching the lesson.

Essentially, at least at first, you may be modelling the planning of the lesson, using the lesson resources, such as a booklet, to make annotations and notes and asking your team to follow and contribute. As this journey continues, the collaboration should develop and you may want to start asking others within your team to lead different sessions to help to draw on specific expertise within your department, and to develop their leadership too.

Co-planning means that you are ensuring that everyone is getting the best ideas, and that all the students are getting the best of every teacher in your team.

Intervention

Case Study: Duncan Stokes, Teacher of English

Intervention

Through my years of teaching, I have been asked to teach intervention sessions to students: mainly those in YII but also to YI0 on occasion. Intervention groups have been either voluntary to students and been after school; voluntary to students at lunchtime; compulsory to students at lunchtime in small groups of four to five; compulsory to students after school in a variety of sized groups from five to ten students.

In my experience, the voluntary ones were attended by students whose parents asked them to go and were wholly ineffective. Staff morale on such events was low due to being at the end of a long teaching day and the sessions were impossible to prepare for effectively as there was no knowledge of who, if any, students would arrive. Moreover, those students who were there, were lacking motivation due to losing their own valuable free time.

Compulsory sessions were clearly better attended; more planning was possible due to knowing who was (theoretically) going to be there. Motivation of both staff and students again was not 100% due to encroachment on valuable free time. Why were these students selected? Students were selected based on data from previous assessments: these four students all got 5s in their mocks but need 7s. Clearly, these four students have individual intervention needs to go from five to seven. In my setting, these students were chosen by a non-subject specialist member of SLT. These sessions effectively turn into a normal lesson with questioning being used to elicit responses and ideas from students to help the others. Rarely did students share some, if any, similar areas on which they needed to improve. For example, I had a student with great textual knowledge who needed support with punctuation and syntax; another had great knowledge but needed to hone planning an essay; another needed to learn supportive textual reference; another needed to connect ideas into a more honed thesis; yet another need to draw out the relevance of the writers' methodology. The list goes on. The aforementioned teaching and individual needs are concepts which have previously been taught throughout the students' learning and have, in a group situation (a classroom), not been mastered.

Teachers know what each student needs to do: teachers need intensive intervention with an individual student so that they can master a skill which has hitherto eluded them.

Intervention is a really difficult area in education. We all want students to do well in their exams, of course, but all too often we see sticking plaster intervention coming in at the very end of their education journey. This is too late! Intervention needs to be an ongoing process from Year 7. As we discuss in our chapter on assessment, there needs to be ongoing diagnostic formative assessment that pinpoints exactly what the students don't know so that this can be retaught. When we have generic, grade-based intervention, such as that described in the case study above, we find that this is too broad to make the intervention effective, and this means that we are wasting time – our most precious commodity.

Of course, there will probably need to be intervention in the examination years, because it is, indeed, ongoing, and we won't have fixed everything in the earlier years no matter how hard we have tried. However, what we need to try and do, as middle leaders, is to make it more worthwhile. SLT will be making some decisions here no doubt, based on grades, but you can assert some influence too as the subject specialist which will be really helpful for them. Use question-level analysis, and careful diagnostic testing, or even qualitative research through conversations with classroom teachers, to identify the specific needs of the students regardless of the grade. Then you can group students into areas that can be tackled with deliberate and focused practice, and direct your team towards their most expert areas too.

Teaching and learning top tips

- Use cognitive science as a basis for your understanding; it is the best bet we have for understanding how learning works.

- Make sure that all of the students are thinking about the right thing.

- Make sure all of the students are thinking!

- Make sure that students are thinking hard and that learning is slowed down so that core knowledge is mastered.

- Introduce teaching and learning techniques to your team gradually and embed each one before starting another.

- Always make time for teaching and learning in your department meetings.

- Have co-planning sessions regularly to ensure a shared understanding of what, why and how you are teaching your curriculum.

- Make intervention regular, ongoing and specific.

Notes

1 Furst, E. (2021). *EfratFurst – Learning in the brain*. [online] Sites.google.com. Available at: https://sites.google.com/view/efratfurst/learning-in-the-brain [Accessed 8 June 2021].

2 Sweller, J. (1988). Cognitive Load during Problem Solving: Effects on Learning. Cognitive Science, 12, pp. 257–285.

3 Image by David Goodwin adapted from Furst, E. (2021). *EfratFurst - Learning in the brain*. [online] Sites.google.com. Available at: https://sites.google.com/view/efratfurst/learning-in-the-brain [Accessed 8 June 2021].

4 Furst, E. (2021). *EfratFurst - Learning in the brain*. [online] Sites.google.com. Available at: https://sites.google.com/view/efratfurst/learning-in-the-brain [Accessed 8 June 2021].

5 OFSTED. (2009). *English at the Crossroads*. London: Crown.

6 Didau, D. (2019). *Skill = knowledge + practice*. [online] David Didau. Available at: https://learningspy.co.uk/learning/you-cant-teach-skills/ [Accessed 15 June 2021].

7 Image by David Goodwin.

8 Bjork, R. (2012). *Using our memory shapes our memory*. [video] Available at: http://gocognitive.net/interviews/using-our-memory-shapes-our-memory [Accessed 28 August 2021].

9 Lemov, D. (2015). Teach Like a Champion 2.0 – 62 Techniques that put students on the path to college, Jossey-Bass, USA.

10 Bjork, E. and Bjork, R. (2011). 'Making things hard on yourself, but in a good way: Creating desirable difficulties to enhance learning'. Gernsbacher M, Pew R, Hough L, et al. (eds) *Psychology and the Real World: Essays Illustrating Fundamental Contributions to Society*. New York: Worth, pp. 55–64.

11 Willingham, D. (2008). *What Will Improve a Student's Memory?*. American Educator, Winter 2008–2009, https://www.aft.org/sites/default/files/periodicals/willingham_0.pdf.

12 Bjork, E. L. and Bjork, R. A. (2015). Making things hard on yourself, but in a good way: Creating desirable difficulties to enhance learning. In Gernsbacher, M. A., Pomerantz, J. R. (Eds.), Psychology and the real world: Essays illustrating fundamental contributions to society (2nd ed., pp. 55–64). New York, NY: Worth.

13 Land, R., Cousin, G., Meyer, J.H.F., and Davies, P. (2005). Threshold concepts and troublesome knowledge (3): implications for course design and evaluation, in C. Rust (ed.), Improving Student Learning – equality and diversity, Oxford: OCSLD.

14 Howard, K. and Hill, C. (2020). *Symbiosis*. Melton: John Catt, pp. 67–72.

15 Howard, K. and Hill, C. (2020). *Symbiosis*. Melton: John Catt, p. 69.

16 Howard, K. and Hill, C. (2020). *Symbiosis*. Melton: John Catt, p. 70.

17 Willingham, Daniel, T. (2009). *Why don't students like school?* Jossey-Bass. p. 79

18 Lemov, D. (2015). *Teach Like a Champion 2.0 – 62 Techniques that put students on the path to college*, Jossey-Bass, USA.

19 BAMBRICH-SANTOYO, P. (2018). *Leverage Leadership 2.0*: A Practical Guide to Building Exceptional Schools. San Francisco: Jossey-Bass. p. 55.

20 Lemov, D. (2015). Teach Like a Champion 2.0 – 62 Techniques that put students on the path to college, Jossey-Bass, USA.

21 Coe, R. (2013). *Improving Education: A Triumph of Hope Over Experience, CEM Inaugural Lecture.* Available at http://www.cem.org/attachments/publications/ImprovingEducation2013.pdf.

22 Lemov, D. (2015). Teach Like a Champion 2.0 – 62 Techniques that put students on the path to college, Jossey-Bass, USA.

Bibliography

Bambrich-Santoyo, P. (2018). *Leverage Leadership 2.0: A Practical Guide to Building Exceptional Schools*. San Francisco: Jossey-Bass.

Bjork E., & Bjork R. (2011). "Making things hard on yourself, but in a good way: Creating desirable difficulties to enhance learning," in Gernsbacher M., Pew R., Hough L., et al. (eds) *Psychology and the Real World: Essays Illustrating Fundamental Contributions to Society*. New York: Worth, pp. 55–64.

Bjork, R. (2012). *Using our memory shapes our memory.* [video] Available at: http://gocognitive.net/interviews/using-our-memory-shapes-our-memory [Accessed 28 August 2021].

Bjork, E. L., & Bjork, R. A. (2015). "Making things hard on yourself, but in a good way: Creating desirable difficulties to enhance learning". in Gernsbacher, M. A., Pomerantz, J. R. (Eds.), *Psychology and the real world: Essays illustrating fundamental contributions to society* (2nd ed., pp. 55–64). New York, NY: Worth.

Chun, B., & Ja, H. (2018). *Figure 1. Ebbinghaus' forgetting curve and review cycle.* [online] ResearchGate. Available at: https://www.researchgate.net/figure/Ebbinghaus-forgetting-curve-and-review-cycle_fig1_324816198 [Accessed 17 June 2021].

Coe, R. (2013). *Improving Education: A Triumph of Hope Over Experience, CEM Inaugural Lecture.* Available http://www.cem.org/attachments/publications/ImprovingEducation2013.pdf

Didau, D. (2019). *Skill = knowledge + practice.*[online] David Didau. Available at: https://learningspy.co.uk/learning/you-cant-teach-skills/ [Accessed 15 June 2021].

Furst, E. (2021). *EfratFurst – Learning in the brain.* [online] Sites.google.com. Available at: https://sites.google.com/view/efratfurst/learning-in-the-brain [Accessed 8 June 2021].

Howard, K., & Hill, C. (2020) *Symbiosis.* Melton: John Catt.

Land, R., Cousin, G., Meyer, J. H. F., & Davies, P. (2005). Threshold concepts and troublesome knowledge (3): implications for course design and evaluation, in C. Rust (ed.), *Improving Student Learning – Equality and Diversity.* Oxford: OCSLD.

Lemov, D. (2015). *Teach Like a Champion 2.0 – 62 Techniques that put students on the path to college.* USA: Jossey-Bass.

OFSTED. (2009). *English at the Crossroads.* London: Crown.

Sweller, J. (1988). "Cognitive load during problem solving: effects on learning". *Cognitive Science*, 12, p. 257–285.

Willingham, D. (2008). *What Will Improve a Student's Memory?.* American Educator, Winter 2008-2009, https://www.aft.org/sites/default/files/periodicals/willingham_0.pdf.

Willingham, Daniel T. (2009). *Why Don't Students Like School?* Jossey-Bass.

7 Assessment

As a leader of curriculum or cohort, you will be motivated by, and accountable for, the progress of the students in your subject/year/Key Stage/House. This means that you need to know if they have learned what you wanted them to learn, and then act on it: this is assessment.

When we deal with the complexities of assessment, it is very easy to get things wrong. Indeed, many whole-school systems make getting it right rather difficult! However, armed with the knowledge of the theory of assessment, its core purpose, features and practical ideas on how to put these into action, even in one of these schools, you can be the force for positive change in your school.

The two main concepts that are important to understand in assessment are validity and reliability. Arguably, validity is the most important, so let's deal with that first.

Validity

As we have discussed frequently throughout this book, the subject you lead as a middle leader of curriculum is paramount to everything you do, because it has a specific domain of knowledge and expertise. It is important to remember, and regard these, as constructs – that being something which is societally created, having specific traits that we expect to see that will define being 'good' in that subject. For example, in science, building up knowledge of the different areas of scientific processes and methods of enquiry, being able to understand how different areas of the subject, such as photosynthesis, respiration and chemical reactions interlink. Or in art, developing a broad knowledge of different artistic styles and techniques until being ultimately able to manipulate these in creating and evaluating complex pieces of art and understanding how art shapes and reflects society.

Therefore, our first point in assessment aligns with that in curriculum development – defining the specific set of knowledge that makes up the construct of your subject, because this is what you need to assess for, as well as teach. So, one aspect of validity is whether a test or assessment assesses what it claims or aims to,

 DOI: 10.4324/9781003160557-8

as Dylan Wiliam tells us, an assessment 'must address all important aspects of the construct about which we wish to generalise'.[1] And generalise is what an assessment indeed does if we are using it to make a judgement about how 'good' a student is in our subject; we are using the assessment as a sample of the learning in the hope that it reflects the wider construct of the curriculum we have created. This is a double-faceted validation of both your curriculum and the assessment, since the content of the assessment can only represent the construct if the curriculum does so too. Also, it is important to note here that it is not just the assessment itself that we need to consider in terms of validity, it is also the way that we use the information we glean from this assessment. Kane's definition of validity mainly, in fact, focuses on this, saying that validity is about the inferences that are drawn from assessment results, and the way they are interpreted; it is 'the extent to which the evidence supports or refutes the proposed interpretations and uses' of assessment results.[2]

It is imperative to identify, before anything else, the purpose of your assessment. An assessment is only valid if it fulfils its purpose: for example, the purpose of the GCSE examinations is to certify a level of learning in the construct of a specific subject domain. However, the purpose of the assessments that lead up to that will be very different, although they will still need to maintain high validity. Messick defines validity as 'an integrated evaluative judgement of the degree to which empirical evidence and theoretical rationales support the adequacy and appropriateness of inferences and actions based on the test scores or other modes of assessment',[3] meaning that, in order for an assessment to be valid, we must be able to judge that the inferences we make from the assessment are valid representations of the construct it seeks to assess. Messick identified two major threats to validity: construct under-representation and construct irrelevant variance.[4]

To avoid construct under-representation, we must look carefully at the breadth of the assessment's content; if we wish to know how well our Year 7 cohort have learned the content of the whole Year 7 curriculum, it will not be representative to only ask about the final unit from the year. There should be a representative sample from all of the important knowledge you have identified for that stage of your curriculum so that the inferences you draw give the clearest picture of their learning across the whole year.

In order to minimise construct irrelevant variance, we need to think carefully about the types of questions we ask and whether they are the next representations of the construct we wish to assess. For example, although the subject domains of English and history share several aspects of substantive knowledge (factual historical knowledge in context for texts, for example) and procedural knowledge (essay writing), we must ensure that our assessment focuses on the subject we wish to assess: asking our students, in an English assessment, to write an account of witch trials as part of their assessment on Macbeth would not have high construct relevance, for example, even though knowledge of witches and witch trials is important for the study of this text, the writing of an account would not be relevant for the construct of literary study.

Reliability

Next, we want to try to maximise the reliability of our assessment. Validity and reliability are linked, but whilst it is not possible to have an assessment that is valid but not reliable (because we would be unable to make the right inferences from it), it is possible to have an assessment that is reliable but not valid, not that we would want to! This is because a result can be numerically reliable independent of what it is actually testing. Reliability essentially means that something is consistent, that the same result would occur repeatedly regardless of who was producing it. Neil Jones[5] uses an analogy of train punctuality to perfectly illustrate this idea, explaining that a train service can be late consistently, and this would mean that the late train was actually highly reliable in its lateness. However, the result itself is not accurate – it is not arriving at the correct time. This is the same with assessment; a group of markers could reliably put a group into the same rank order, giving them very similar marks even though they are not accurate in terms of what we want to measure, but for a test to be valid, we do need to have some degree of reliability in order to make the inferences of the results meaningful.

So, whilst validity is our primary purpose, we do want to have high reliability to enhance this. We can use a formula, Classical Test Theory,[6] to help us to understand how to achieve this better:

"True score" = achieved score + /−error

In this formula, the 'true score' is in fact theoretical – it is something that we never actually know, but represents what the student should have got in the test. The achieved score is the mark that they actually received, which is of course affected by error. In order to ensure that the achieved score is as close as possible to the true score, which would mean that the test was sound in making inferences about a student's knowledge in that area, we want the error to be as little as possible. When we talk about 'error' here, we don't mean mistakes such as adding up the numbers wrong (although this would obviously negatively affect reliability too), but rather the factors which may create variance in the achieved score. Dr Paul Newton gives possible sources of error including the occasion (sitting the test on different days could return different results), the test itself (due to confusing wording in questions for example, or choice of topic), the person marking the test (a different person may not recognise and award the same features or answers), and the level- or grade-setting panel (a different team of people may have set different thresholds to attain each level or grade).[7]

In order to minimise error, we want to control as many of these sources as we can. The occasion, and how different students perform on this occasion, is difficult to manage, but we can try to maintain a standard by ensuring that administration and conditions are uniform, for example by having all students sit the assessment at the same time and with the same scaffolding, preparation, etc, to make this as even as possible. In devising the test itself, we can exert a lot of control by being careful and particular about our wording, question selection, marks awarded and physical construction. For marking, it is imperative that we minimise error by having stringent training and moderation for our marking teams in order that we are applying the same standard, and having that checked and monitored across the cohort. Level-setting is something that can, in Key Stage 3 at least, be avoided entirely. By adding in grade or levels or colours or fruit or whatever method your school decides to try and group students, it is going to reduce reliability, because it is adding another layer of arbitration when deciding on boundaries for these, so it will be more reliable to report only a score, or percentage. For Key Stages 4 and 5, there will need to be careful consideration over which boundaries to apply, and whether it is really necessary on most assessments. By looking at the examination board's decisions and echoing their parameters, it is likely to make decisions in this area less likely to increase error.

Key Stage 3 assessment

As previously stated, many establishments have whole-school, or even trust-wide, systems which can be detrimental to validity and reliability, which is particularly evident in Key Stage 3 assessment. After the removal of levels in Key Stage 3 in 2014, this key stage was the only one left with no external accountability measure for core subjects, which left many schools feeling lacking in direction. This led to internal measures being brought in that felt, at the time, like the most logical and sensible things to bridge this gap and help us to see how students were progressing towards GCSE: the use of GCSE grading from Year 7. Although this was a nice way to track data, it was not reliable or valid as the GCSE criteria and grading systems that created these grades did not match the curriculum being taught. They might give a clear 'flightpath' for stakeholders to try and predict and monitor progress towards GCSE, but mainly they used grade descriptors that did not actually match up to the raw marking system that is actually used to determine grades at GCSE: basically, this was made up nonsense created to feed a data monster. Many used different systems, such as always reporting the predicted grade based on the current performance, or even using a word such as 'expected', or 'exceeding'; such variety of methods meant that this was even more pointless since the people whom this data was really for, the teachers and the parents, often did not understand it! Remember that we must always consider the purpose of an assessment first, and at Key Stage 3, we need to know what the students know, and how they are getting on in comparison to the rest of the cohort. This means that the assessment must have an impact on teaching and learning, and any assessment in Key Stage 3 that does not have an impact on teaching and learning is pointless.

This point coincides with the use of exam board-generated papers for use in Key Stage 3 assessment. It may seem like a positive move to train your cohort up as soon as possible in the style of exam so that they can get as much practice as possible before the real event. However, what is really being learned here? In many subjects, the content will be different from the GCSE course, and students need to have the foundations of other knowledge before they can tackle the types of questions that they will be presented with at GCSE. Also, what are the students really learning in completing practice papers like this? This is really surface-level teaching; they are learning how to pass the exam, but are they really learning your subject? Using these types of assessments will reduce the validity of your assessments and produce false results. The feedback from these assessments is likely to be quite generic and focus on quick wins since the pressure to show progress on the next practice paper is high; it will not be focused and diagnostic. Moreover, repeatedly training by doing the same style of paper again, and learning how to complete an exam, rather than learning about your beautiful and interesting subject, is dull! It saps all the love of the subject that you want to create and inspire in your students, and that would create real and valid learning and attainment.

Assessment design

When designing a curriculum, we need to be very conscious of how we are going to assess it – how well have the students learned what we wanted them to learn? We know that, to use assessment guru Daisy Christodoulou's analogy, you don't prepare for a marathon by running marathons – you do sprints, fartlek, long runs, intervals, short runs – all designed to prepare you for the marathon in different ways.[8] This relates to exam technique; it is important, but it must come right at the end, when students have been taught what they need to know first. So how, without the exam-style tasks we used to use to 'assess', how do we assess instead?

Firstly, we need to ensure we use precise and targeted assessment tasks: essay writing, for example, whilst often a key element of exams in many subjects, provides so much information and tests so many skills that it becomes difficult to know where the common misconceptions are. Is this error here a fundamental misunderstanding of a concept, or just a mistake? Essays are a scattergun, imprecise approach, which often also rely on mark schemes that describe where students are right now, not how to move them forward; that is possibly the best way for exam boards to sample and assess the whole domain, (and by domain here we're talking about the curriculum), in a summative fashion, for as Christodoulou says,

> The domain that tests are trying to measure is the extent of a pupil's knowledge and skills and their ability to apply these skills. ... The domain is vast, and normally we have just a two or three-hour exam to try and measure this domain.[9]

However, it's not appropriate for formative use when we need precise information to tell us where common misconceptions are, what has not been understood, what has not been taught effectively and what needs re-teaching.

Assessment and the curriculum

This brings us onto talking more about the curriculum, and how that links, intrinsically, with testing. In Christodoulou's words, 'In order for the test to provide a valid inference about how a pupil will perform on the entire domain, teaching must be geared towards the domain'.[10] This is why, as discussed in the chapters on curriculum, our curriculum design needs to be focussed not on a presumed endpoint: the test, the GCSE, the A-Level, but on teaching the most important knowledge from the domain. The school KS3 curriculum can't ever be the whole domain, but it is significantly wider than GCSE summative assessments. And ultimately, the test isn't why we came into teaching: it wasn't to train students to pass a GCSE at Grade 4, although that is important, but to instil a love of our subject.

We need to assess students' progress – what they know and can do – but grading is not the way to do so. The curriculum itself is the progression model: by knowing each part of the curriculum and moving forwards to the next knowledge, students are progressing. Our assessments need to check that our students do know each part of the curriculum, what they do not know and, as a result, what we need to reteach them.

Therefore, if the curriculum is our progression model, flight paths and age-related standards do not work, because they don't allow us to understand what progress an individual student is making in mastering the key knowledge of the domain i.e. the curriculum. And as we have said before, this use of descriptors describes a snapshot of student work but doesn't tell us what they (or we) need to do to move them forward.

To return to the thrust of what we are talking about, if we have designed our curriculum as a coherent, sequenced progression through that domain knowledge, then we need to test their mastery of that knowledge. And to keep testing it, to ensure that they have retained it over time. As David Didau says simply but eloquently:

> Using the curriculum as a progression model simply means that we make judgements of progress based on how much of the curriculum a child has learned. The more carefully we have specified what we intend to teach, the more easily we can assess whether they've learned it.[11]

What this means then is that we have to have expectations of students' mastery of our curriculum. If they do not meet those expectations then from our precise assessment of their domain knowledge we can diagnose the root of the issue: have MOST students misunderstood that Fagin is a villain? If so, the curriculum is at fault and we need to redesign that element of the scheme. If just my class have failed to understand that Fagin is a villain, then I have not taught it effectively, and I need to reflect on and adapt my approach, and seek advice from my colleagues. Or is it a small demographic of students who haven't understood it? In that case, do they need a particular level of extra and specific support – not what we used to call differentiation by a different worksheet, or an all, most, some task, but perhaps targeted questioning or PSA support for the re-teach task. In all of this, it is the teacher who acts on this assessment feedback, not the student.

Formative assessment types

A practical way of assessing formatively is through multiple-choice quizzing. This can be completed at regular intervals to inform teaching (as well as helping to secure knowledge though the testing effect). In devising these, we can create stronger validity by ensuring that the questions cover the breadth of the content of the curriculum taught in the specified time period that the quiz is assessing, such as two weeks; by using your knowledge mapping from your curriculum creation, as well as discussion and feedback from the teachers in your team, you can ensure that the construct representation is high by sticking to the knowledge that you have specified as important. Reducing construct irrelevant variance may appear more challenging, but consider how to adapt your questions to represent the important aspects of your subject: although a multiple choice question may be most useful for checking retention of substantive knowledge, they can also be used to check disciplinary knowledge and procedural knowledge: could a source be provided with different options about the reliability of this information in an history assessment? Could a quotation be provided, with different options for interpretation and inferences in an English assessment? By carefully designing these questions, we can keep our validity high whilst maintaining precision and practicality, as well as reducing workload. Also, through using standardised multiple choice quizzes, we can carefully control the reliability of our assessments by working as a team to ensure that wording and format are accessible for all in order to minimise error in terms of the test itself. We can also achieve high reliability in terms of marking since with this type of question, the answer is either right or wrong, and there is no error margin for human judgement involved.

Remember that formative assessment is not always quite so formal as it may seem here. Indeed, most of your formative assessment will be constant and ongoing within the classroom. Every time you ask a question and cold-call a student to answer it, you are assessing. Make sure that you use this opportunity as effectively as you can. Sometimes we should cold-call virtually 'at random', as this will give us a good sample of the room; in your head, of course, you will probably want to be selecting a few students who represent different areas of your cohort, and you will be making inferences based on their answers, and perhaps then probing deeper to pinpoint misconceptions that may have arisen so that you can deal with them there and then, before they are embedded. This can be a particularly powerful tool when you are aware of gaps in knowledge, perhaps from more formal quizzes, or previous questioning, and you can surreptitiously look at your notes on this before directing your question to the student you need to check with.

A highly effective tool for gauging whole-class understanding for instant formative assessment is the mini-whiteboard. With clear and precise routines (such as ensuring boards are revealed in unison when a signal is given to avoid clouding reliability due to students copying their peers' responses), you can have an instant measure of a class's progress with an activity, or across a lesson. An equation, a formula, a grammar exercise, an example of new vocabulary, or any substantive knowledge would be perfect for this activity. We would recommend always having paper and pen in hand when asking student to show you an answer on their mini-whiteboard – this means that you can note down the specific students who have misconceptions, perhaps grouping them into the types of misconception, and then take action – ask them to try again with feedback, question them further to see where they went wrong and why, or target them for more in-depth reteaching and follow-up cold-calling later in the lesson, and next lesson. However, what your mini-whiteboard exercise may reveal is that a lot of students have not got this right in which case you need to spend time reteaching right now to the whole class.

Most important in all of these cases are the inferences and actions we make from our formative assessments. Formative assessment is responsive, adaptive teaching, a deliberate mapping of what good teachers do in the classroom all the time, but when designing a curriculum it needs harnessing to assess the effectiveness of the curriculum e.g. what's the result of the fortnightly quiz? Are there patterns across all classes which point to a problem in the curriculum?

To return to our original focus on assessment and the curriculum: If we have designed a well-sequenced curriculum, we assess progress by asking are students progressing through the domain: how much of what I wanted them to learn this year have they learnt?

Summative assessment types

Again when we are considering summative assessment, our focus needs to be on the purpose of the assessment. This will depend on the stage the assessment is taken at, and also the stakeholder, so both of these things need to be considered when deciding how to make our summative assessments most effective.

Summative assessments will largely have the purpose of rank-ordering the cohort so that progress can be reported to different stakeholders. SLT will generally want to know how the cohort is progressing as a whole. Parents and guardians will want to know how their child is getting on in comparison to others. Teachers will want to know how their classes are doing. As a middle leader with responsibility and accountability, your needs are the greatest here; you will need to know all of these things and more, so you need to consider the best way for the assessment to service these needs.

In Key Stage 3, as we have already said, we don't want to be using pretend GCSE assessments, but to be precisely checking the knowledge that has been learned. This is the most effective priority for teaching and learning. We can complete this through a mixture of multiple choice, short answer and more extended questions which match the stage of procedural knowledge you wish to assess. When devising the assessment, you need to think carefully about not under-representing the content of your curriculum, so choosing the questions is important. It is also imperative to carefully check that the question wording is not confusing: does that question wording mean that the students are actually having to decipher vocabulary that has not been explicitly taught to them? If so, you may not be actually assessing the knowledge that you want to check, but rather the vocabulary they have learned at home, which means that your validity will be adversely affected. Once an assessment has been devised, you will need to consider your mark scheme. How much is each of the questions worth? How important and valuable is each piece of knowledge that you are assessing? This should be reflected in the number of marks it is given. When you are further on in your Key Stage 3 curriculum, and are able to test more extended pieces which match up to the array of knowledge which has hopefully been mastered at this stage, your mark scheme will need to reflect the increased difficulty in these sections. It will also need to provide as much clarity as possible for those marking the assessment on how to award the marks: are there specific keywords that need to be included? What specific criteria need to be met for each piece of procedural knowledge to be deemed successful? Providing extremely precise criteria, as well as examples and non-examples, will increase reliability as there is less margin for marker error.

Comparative judgement

Another valuable tool in the assessing of more extended pieces is the use of comparative judgement as advocated for by Daisy Christodolou, particularly on the platform www.nomoremarking.com,[12] although comparative judgement can take place without this. Comparative judgement is becoming an increasingly popular method of assessment and it's exciting to see an increasing number of schools embracing this process.

It is not natural for us to come to an absolute judgement on a singular piece of work, particularly with the more subjective subjects and with longer discursive pieces of work, and it is much easier for us to be able to compare two examples in order to make a judgement on quality. Even with the most detailed training on rubrics, exam board expectations and annotation tracking, it is highly unlikely that a team of examiners will agree on the overall mark for a piece of work. Statistics suggest that the likelihood of examiners consistently reaching the 'definitive' mark (the grade agreed by the most senior examiner) is low, with a trial showing that just 28% of original marks were agreed upon by other examiners with the same training[13]; this is not a promising figure for the reliability of this type of marking.

Comparative judgement 'offers a radical alternative to the pursuit of reliability through detailed mark schemes'[14] and an 'elegant solution'[15] to the often laborious task of marking and annotating essay by essay. By placing two assessments side by side, teachers are able to use their expertise to decide which of the pieces is the better piece of work. And because this way of assessing is more natural to the way our brains work, comparative judgement is proven to be more reliable, have high validity and be more efficient than traditional methods of essay marking.[16] In fact, 'research has shown the process to be as reliable as double marking, but much quicker'.[17] Therefore, if we move away from the more mark-scheme-based style of judging assessments and step towards comparing them, then our rank order (which is essentially what all marking and grading is) will be more reliable. If our assessment is more reliable, then the information that we draw from them about our students and their learning is going to be too. And if we are using our expertise as subject specialists, with our delicate understanding of the construct of our subjects, then our judgements, inferences, and therefore our assessments should also have high validity, which is the most important aspect of assessment.

Quality assurance and reporting

So that Key Stage 3 assessments can perform their roles for other stakeholders, we can use percentages to show the overall success of each student: this is useful for you, and SLT, who can then see how much of the curriculum has been mastered and retained. For parents and guardians, there will need to be a comparative aspect so that they can see how their own child is getting on comparatively to others so that they can support; reporting an average percentage for comparison is a wise idea here, as it should show these stakeholders whether their child is in line, below, or exceeding the average.

In Keys Stages 4 and 5, we will want to start using summative assessments that are closer to the actual examinations that they will be sitting. This is easier in terms of the construction of assessments, since past papers are available that should be perfectly representative of that point of sampling the subject domain. There will also be mark schemes available that will aid your precision here. However, there is, particularly in subjects that are known to be more subjective such as English, a lot of skill in interpreting and applying the mark scheme. This is why it is imperative to meet as a whole team beforehand and look at examples so that you are applying the mark scheme in as uniform a way as possible. If you are lucky enough to have examiners on your team, or even better senior examiners who will be experienced in deciding on how the marks are applied and in training examiners, then it would be wise to enlist them to conduct this training as this will produce the most valid and reliable results for all stakeholders.

Similarly, after the marking has been completed, there should be some stringent moderation so that you can ensure that there is equality and uniformity in the distribution of marks. Sampling of papers by senior examiners, examiners, or, if they are not available, yourself should be thorough and cover the full spectrum of teachers and marks. You can then spot trends and see if marks need to be adjusted. There is no point in assessing the whole cohort in a summative manner if the results are not compared robustly as this will mean that students are receiving inaccurate and inadequate feedback, much like the data you will have generated for the other stakeholders and yourself.

Even though these assessments are summative, that does not mean we should ignore the inferences that we make from them. By analysing question, class and student-level data, we can make some formative use of these assessments too. If all of the cohort have done badly in one area, then how can you reteach this to ensure that they understand it? And how can you address the planning and teaching of this area in your department so that next year's cohort do not suffer the same misconceptions? If certain classes have performed less well than others in specific areas, then this can give you valuable information about the training needs of your department. Similarly, if some classes have excelled, this can give you valuable insight into which teachers would be ideal for giving the department some training in this and sharing their expertise! Student-level data can be important for providing an overall picture about students of concern, and useful for pastoral leaders to collate.

Any assessment needs to have purpose, and all assessments should have an impact on teaching and learning.

Top tips for assessment

- Make sure your assessment only assesses what you have taught up to that point.

- Make sure your assessment represents all of the knowledge that you need to check mastery of.

- Make sure your assessment focuses on your own subject's knowledge, and doesn't become muddled with others.

- For formative assessment, ensure that your assessment allows you to precisely diagnose the knowledge that needs to be retaught.

- Use percentages in Key Stage 3 to report overall progress, with comparison to an average percentage for guardians.

- In Key Stages 4 and 5, use senior examiners and examiners for training, standardisation and moderation to ensure accuracy and rigour if at all possible.

- Act on the results of all of your assessments: how can the inferences you make affect the learning for this cohort and the following ones?

Notes

1 William, D. (2008). 'Quality in assessment' in Swaffield, S. (ed.) *Unlocking Assessment.* London: Routledge, Chapter 8 p. 128.
2 Kane, M.T. (2006). Validation. In R.L. Brennan (Ed). *Educational Measurement* (4th edition) (pp. 17–64). Washington, DC: American Council on Education/Praeger, p. 17.
3 Messick, S. (1989). 'Validity' in R. L. Linn (ed.) *Educational Measurement* (3rd ed.) Old Tappen, NJ: Macmillan, p. 13.
4 Ibid.
5 Jones, N. (2012). *Reliability and Dependability* in Fulcher, G. and Davidson, F. (Eds.) *The Routledge Book of Language Testing*, London: Routledge, p. 352.
6 Frey, B. (2018). *The SAGE encyclopedia of educational research, measurement, and evaluation* (Vols. 1–4). Thousand Oaks, CA: SAGE Publications, Inc. doi: 10.4135/97815 06326139
7 Newton, Paul E. (2008). *Recognising the error of our ways* Presentation to the Cambridge Assessment Forum for New Developments in Educational Assessment. Downing College, Cambridge. 10 December 2008. https://www.cambridgeassessment.org.uk/insights/ concept-of-error/
8 Christodoulou, D. (2017). *Making Good Progress?: The Future of Assessment for Learning*. Oxford University Press-Children, p. 156.
9 Christodoulou, D. (2014). *Why teaching to the test is so bad - Daisy Christodoulou.* [online] Daisy Christodoulou. Available at: https://daisychristodoulou.com/2014/01/ why-teaching-to-the-test-is-so-bad/ [Accessed 13 January 2021].
10 Ibid.
11 Didau, D. (2020). *Curriculum related expectations: using the curriculum as a progression model.* [online] David Didau. Available at: https://learningspy.co.uk/assessment/ curriculum-related-expectations/ [Accessed 19 January 2021].
12 No More Marking. (2020). *No More Marking.* [online] Nomoremarking.com. Available at: https://www.nomoremarking.com/ [Accessed 19 July 2021].
13 OFQUAL. (2016). *Reviews of marking and moderation for GCSE and GCE: summer 2016 exam series.* London: Crown.
14 Pollitt, A. (2012). The method of adaptive comparative judgement, assessment in education: principles, *Policy & Practice*, *19*(3), 281–300, DOI: 10.1080/0969594X.2012.665354.
15 Christodoulou, D. (2015). *Comparative judgment: 21st century assessment – Daisy Christodoulou.* [online] Daisy Christodoulou. Available at: https://daisychristodoulou. com/2015/11/comparative-judgment-21st-century-assessment/ [Accessed 19 July 2021].
16 Marshall, N., Shaw, K., Hunter, J., and Jones, I. (2020). Assessment by comparative judgement: an application to secondary statistics and English in New Zealand. *New Zealand Journal of Educational Studies*, *55*(1), pp. 49–71.
17 No More Marking. (2020). *No More Marking.* [online] Nomoremarking.com. Available at: https://www.nomoremarking.com/ [Accessed 19 July 2021].

Bibliography

Christodoulou, D. (2014). *Why teaching to the test is so bad – Daisy Christodoulou.* [online] Daisy Christodoulou. Available at: https://daisychristodoulou.com/2014/01/why-teaching-to-the-test-is-so-bad/ [Accessed 13 January 2021].

Christodoulou, D. (2015). *Comparative judgment: 21st century assessment – Daisy Christodoulou*. [online] Daisy Christodoulou. Available at: https://daisychristodoulou. com/2015/11/comparative-judgment-21st-century-assessment/ [Accessed 19 July 2021].

Christodoulou, D. (2017). *Making Good Progress?: The Future of Assessment for Learning.* Oxford University Press-Children.

Didau, D. (2020). *Curriculum related expectations: using the curriculum as a progression model.* [online] David Didau. Available at: https://learningspy.co.uk/assessment/ curriculum-related-expectations/ [Accessed 19 January 2021].

Frey, B. (2018). *The SAGE Encyclopedia of Educational Research, Measurement, and Evaluation* (Vols. 1–4). Thousand Oaks, CA: SAGE Publications, Inc. 10.4135/97815 06326139

Jones, N. (2012). *"Reliability and Dependability"*, in Fulcher, G. and Davidson, F. (Eds.), *The Routledge Book of Language Testing*, London: Routledge, p. 352.

Kane, M.T. (2006). "Validation", in R.L. Brennan (Ed). *Educational Measurement* (4th edition) (pp.17–64). Washington, DC: American Council on Education/Praeger.

Marshall, N., Shaw, K., Hunter, J., and Jones, I. (2020). "Assessment by comparative judgement: an application to secondary statistics and English in New Zealand." *New Zealand Journal of Educational Studies, 55*(1), pp. 49–71.

Messick, S. (1989). "Validity", in R. L. Linn (ed.), *Educational Measurement* (3rd ed.) Old Tappen, NJ: Macmillan.

Newton, Paul E. (2008). *Recognising the error of our ways* Presentation to the Cambridge Assessment Forum for New Developments in Educational Assessment. Downing College, Cambridge. 10 December 2008. https://www.cambridgeassessment.org.uk/insights/ concept-of-error/

Pollitt, A. (2012). "The method of adaptive comparative judgement, assessment in education: principles." *Policy & Practice, 19*(3), pp. 281–300, 10.1080/0969594X.2012.665354.

William, D. (2008). "Quality in assessment", in Swaffield, S. (ed.), *Unlocking Assessment.* London: Routledge.

8 Teaching to the top

If we were to travel back in time to circa 2011 and place ourselves within a classroom setting, we might find ourselves surrounded by whiteboards dedicated only to learning objectives or outcomes (Lyndsay never did work out the difference between the two), Nando's style menus on the board for students to 'choose' their task, and colour-coded independent activities on a far-too-detailed PowerPoint slide, where students were directed towards the task that best suited their ability level. Most of us will be able to relate to at least one of those examples, and many of us will recall the hours spent slaving over said PowerPoints and homework menus, and being proud of our efforts in the aftermath – usually because our middle and senior leaders were leading on and rewarding us for using these strategies in the classroom.

Let us be clear here, nobody is criticising those methods at the time that they were so popular. We all thought that what we were doing was solid differentiation, that we were supporting all those in the class to reach the ability that *they* were capable of. However, when we reconsider this now, it's important to ask ourselves the question: who are *we* to decide what *they* are capable of? Why should a student's KS2 data determine how high they reach? Who are *we* to limit how high we set the bar? Progress is never linear and, as well we know, students never fail to surprise us. This is why we must **teach to the very top, always.**

As middle leaders it means us being 'Unapologetically ambitious, unashamedly academic'[1] in our designing of curriculum, schemes of work, and lesson planning in order to allow our students to reach the 'dizziest of heights'[2] whilst we help them up there. It means holding them at the top until they're stable enough to continue alone. It means providing the safety of guidance and a harness on the way up and *always* checking back. This way, we leave nobody behind, we avoid 'the soft bigotry of low expectations'[3] and we show our students – and the staff we lead – that we believe in them regardless of their backgrounds, which in turn creates relationships built on the solidity of mutual respect and trust.

DOI: 10.4324/9781003160557-9

Expertise

As the expert in the room, our teachers are a bounty of knowledge that students must grow from. As middle leaders in charge of developing our teachers, it is imperative we ensure that each of our teachers is trained sufficiently in their subject and that we acknowledge that the process of being a subject specialist does not stop with the gaining of a university degree. On a recent social media poll[4] via Twitter, 87.2% of responding teachers said that they have learnt more about their subject whilst on the job than they did in their university undergraduate studies.

As middle leaders we must fight for time to develop subject knowledge (and for more on this, see the chapter on CPD), in order to ensure that we have teachers who believe themselves to be experts in their field, who can teach our students how to think like experts, read like scholars and communicate all of the above to demonstrate the impact of the quality-first teaching that they receive, day in, day out.

Leading high expectations

Most good schools provide time for subject leaders to have 'curriculum meetings'. However, many of these meetings are that age-old cliché of 'meetings that could have been emails', which we have all seen the notebooks for and not been brave enough to actually take to said meetings. A recurring theme of this book is the finite time that we have as experts both in the classroom, and together as a collegiate network. And it is because of this that we must ensure that every second is spent well. A departmental meeting should not be a run-down of the calendar for the upcoming week, or checking that teachers have all submitted data for the relevant deadlines. Admin is often duplicated via email, so why not just stick to an email bulletin for it instead and use the time provided to meet as a curriculum team to develop subject knowledge, draw on the expertise within your team to develop one another, and co-plan schemes of work so that you can be confident that your team is delivering solid, consistent content to your students? Written down here it makes so much sense, but there are still many schools that haven't yet been able to prioritise subject knowledge development in their directed time calendars, and as a middle leader it's important that you advocate for this to happen. As middle leaders, we are accountable for our team and therefore we are accountable to ensuring that they are always learning, always developing their knowledge and always enjoying the delivery of their subject. Providing time for subject knowledge development is imperative for all three and, if a school you work in isn't doing it, then challenge it; provide a solution to it; and implement change by doing so. Remember that you are not a cog in the machine that simply turns, you are a cog that sticks when things don't work. Your challenge creates change, as explored in the 'Positive Disruption' chapter.

Differentiation

Harking back to the 2010–2020 era, it wasn't uncommon to see all/most/some learning outcomes in every classroom task, Lemon and Herb/Mild and Spicy/Hot style extension menu tasks adorning display boards, and a different level of reading 'challenge' for the same subject in every classroom depending on which set the class was. Top sets in English would be using British Library articles whereas bottom sets would be looking at 'No Fear Shakespeare'. Is it any wonder that there is a consistently wide gap between our SEN/Non SEN, our 'disadvantaged' and 'non-disadvantaged'? It's time to close the chasm and to do so, consistency is absolutely key.

Thinking back to the times of having to develop multiple worksheets for the projected flight path of different students within a class, it could often feel overwhelming and confusing. To our thinking it makes little sense to have different things going on in different classrooms, let alone different things going on in the *same* classroom!

But, if we are always teaching to the top, how do we differentiate? How do we ensure all our students are properly supported? Firstly, for equity, we must agree on a consistent menu of content with our teams. Be that booklets, PowerPoint slides, worksheets, Google Classroom tasks. It doesn't matter. What matters is that it is the same 'spine of the curriculum'[5] with which teachers flex and adapt to suit their students' needs. If we are going to truly provide equity across the diversity of our students within a cohort then we must ensure that the consistency of curriculum is the absolute backbone of every single classroom and, rather than adjusting the content itself, we adjust the level of scaffolding required to support it. This way, we lift students up who would otherwise be dragging along at the bottom, we boost those that are coasting, and we ensure that those who are already attaining highly continue to do so.

Rather than spending hours creating a multitude of resources for all the perceived 'abilities' in a classroom, teachers should be using their time to ensure that their lessons are reflective and responsive. Those hours previously spent colour coding five different worksheets can be used instead (and workload significantly reduced) by looking over a range of classwork, identifying common misconceptions or knowledge not-yet-solidified, and preparing a lesson for all based on that information. That time spent creating differentiated outcome tasks according to prior attainment levels and projected grades can, instead, be spent closely analysing knowledge retrieval responses to identify gaps and target reteaching of certain elements.

Data

With such a focus on data for decades, nobody can blame teachers for making assumptions about a child's future attainment chances based on a spreadsheet of numbers, and sadly we think that forecasted grades based on prior attainment will be around for some time longer. However, GCSE flightpaths and KS3 'GCSE equivalent' grades are misleading; they allow for the passive high attaining students (and, maybe, their teachers too?) to be complacent, and demotivate those that worked hard but didn't perform as well as they might like. Imagine being a student whose GCSE projection in Year 7 is a 3. It doesn't mean much in Year 7, but as the understanding of GCSE grades comes, it is damaging and reductive. On the other hand, imagine being a Year 9 student whose SATs results mean that he is projected to achieve a grade 8. He's coasting because he thinks he can, but is sorely disappointed in Y10 when his mock grade comes out as much lower. What use have these projected grades done for each of these two hypothetical students? Nothing positive, that's for sure. Call them what you want: lowest expected grades, aspirational targets, KS3 to 4 targets... There's no need for the students to know what they are because they provide nothing but a distraction from the truly important thing: learning. Plus, as soon as we attach a grade to a piece of work, it becomes far too easy for the grade to become the sole focus, rather than any feedback about how to approve: '...if a paper is returned with both a grade and a comment, many students will pay attention to the grade and ignore the comment'.[6] (For more on GCSE grades and assessments in KS3 take a look at the chapter on Assessment.)

Of course, we need a guideline as to where the students are at, and where they *could* be heading with the right information, but it is how they are taught that truly determines any future performance. Also, we have to step away from the data for a moment. We are not just teaching these children because they need a number at the end of Y11; we are teaching them the powerful knowledge and expertise that they require to be successful, well-rounded, moral young adults who will lead in all aspects of society in their future. The classrooms that our teams lead in are not exam factories, they are places where children realise what they want to be, who they aspire to and what they want to change.

In order for our classrooms to be all of the above, we must fill them with the 'best that has been thought and said'[7] across all subjects. Of course, we can choose what that material is (as long as it meets the National Curriculum outline as a minimum) but we must question our choices and we absolutely must ensure that, with the material that we deem to be the 'best that has been thought and said', we are creating a level playing field for our students against their peers nationally as well as opening worlds to a diverse array of approaches, opinions and theories.

Practical strategies

If we are asking those with a projected grade four in English Language to 'write a tweet from the perspective of the writer', and those with a projected grade nine to 'summarise how the writer's perspective is portrayed using judicious evidence from the text', we are absolutely not providing a level playing field within our own cohort, let alone against the national picture.

A table of comparison showing a comparison between the approaches of 'damaging differentiation' vs 'teaching to the top'.

Damaging differentiation	Teaching to the top
Target Grade Four and Five: Imagine you are the writer of Source A. Write a tweet explaining how you are feeling (40 character limit).	All students:
	1. Pre-teach any challenging vocabulary.
	2. Read aloud Source A.
Target Grade Six: Find three examples of evidence to prove that the writer of Source A is feeling frustrated with cyclists of his time.	3. Discuss Source A.
	4. Read and annotate the question 'how does the writer of Source A portray their perspective?' (Model this to them, have them copy your model: take contributions from the discussion and note them down as part of your annotations.)
Target Grade Seven+: Summarise how the writer of Source A portrays their perspective, in your own words, drawing on a judicious range of evidence from the text (2–3 paragraphs).	
	5. Now re-read and annotate the text for evidence of perspective (again, model and take parts of the discussion from them as notes).
	6. Model a good answer to the question (I do).
	7. Write a class answer to the question (we do).
	8. Have the students use the above to write their own answer to the question (You do).
	9. Live mark student answers, annotate as you do so, address misconceptions with the whole class.
	10. Review the learning.

Don't get me wrong, the latter approach will take much longer. But better to take the time to do something in detail, to ensure that we intervene where necessary to address misconceptions, and to use a consistent approach to any similar task in order to support students' metacognition. By seeing the process that an expert (their teacher) goes through whilst answering a question, in bite-size 'chunks' for ease of digestion, all students will feel empowered to then replicate the process.

Teaching to the top is the most effective strategy to improve students' confidence and attainment. It is also the strategy which allows teachers to more easily monitor progress, and intervene as necessary to address misconceptions; consistency of approach with this method for similar tasks will significantly support students' metacognition, and 'metacognitive awareness enables control or self-regulation over thinking and learning processes and products'.[8] Through teacher modelling, students can see the process an expert (their teacher) goes through when answering a question, the approach is 'chunked' down for ease of digestion, and as a result they feel empowered to produce the same level of work independently. We teach to the top, we raise aspirations, we build confidence, we motivate via achievement.

This approach may feel very *chalk and talk* which, for many of us who were of the *edutainment* era (where teachers were sometimes referred to as *classroom facilitators*), holds negative connotations due to past expectations to use gimmicks for engagement if we wanted to be anything close to 'good' in a formal lesson observation. So, as a middle leader, implementing this approach to teaching and learning may be challenging. Differentiated outcomes, VAK learning styles and edutainment have rooted deeply within the education sector, and the culture of fear regarding formal lesson observations and OFSTED (prior to the new framework) has made teachers afraid to do something that isn't gimmicky, that may have historically been deemed inadequate for not being 'student-led' enough.

Working as a team

Therefore, in order to get your whole team rowing in the direction that **Teaching to the Top** will take you, you need to get them all on board. Show them, don't just tell them. Provide them with the relevant research about cognitive science principles, present them with case studies of schools whose Progress 8 shows significant improvement in attainment, invite them into your classroom or that of a colleague's where they can see it in practice. As well as using curriculum time to develop our teams' subject knowledge, we must also provide time for pedagogical development.

Top tips for teaching to the top

- The same content in every classroom.

- The curriculum is the progression model.

- Get rid of gimmicks.

- Reflect, respond, reteach.

- Time in the classroom is finite, use it wisely.

- All students deserve access to the very highest of heights.

Notes

1 https://funkypedagogy.wpcomstaging.com/2018/11/04/challenge-for-all-pracped18/
2 *Differentiation Done Well*, 2020 www.hodandheart.co.uk
3 Bush, 2018.
4 https://twitter.com/HoDandHeart/status/1423965103217692673
5 Bawden, L, Brewer, F., Wimbush, H., Hind-Portley, M, Holder, R., Macis-Riley, K., Mann, A., Rowlands, L.M., Sammons. A., Shah, Z., Tsabet, L. (2021). *Succeeding as an English Teacher* London: Bloomsbury.
6 Brookhart, 2008.
7 Arnold, 1894.
8 Hartman, H. J. *Metacognition in Teaching and Learning: An Introduction.*

Bibliography

Arnold, Matthew. (1894). *Culture and Anarchy*. Macmillan.

Brookhart, S. M. (2008). *How to Give Effective Feedback to Your Students*. Association for Supervision and Curriculum Development.

Bush, George. (2000). *Speech to NAACP*. https://georgewbush-whitehouse.archives.gov/news/releases/2006/07/20060720.html

Hartman, Hope J. "Metacognition in Teaching and Learning: An Introduction." *Instructional Science*, *26*(1/2), pp. 1–3.

HoDandHeart. *Differentiation Done Well*. https://hodandheart.co.uk/product/differentiation-done-well/

Mann, A., Bawden, L., Brewer, F., Wimbush, H., Hind-Portley, M., Holder, R., Macis-Riley, K., Rowlands, L. M., Sammons. A., Shah, Z., & Tsabet, L. (2021). *Succeeding as an English Teacher*, London: Bloomsbury.

Webb, Jennifer. "Challenge for All." *Funky Pedagogy*, https://funkypedagogy.wpcomstaging.com/2018/11/04/challenge-for-all-pracped18/

9 Behaviour management

Warm:strict/restorative justice/zero-tolerance, whatever your school's policy is on behaviour, your role as middle leader is to support your team in implementing behaviour management strategies, monitoring and analysing the impact of behaviour on learning, and providing the relevant intervention as the most senior member of staff in your department/year team.

When we talk about behaviour management as educators, it always seems to me that there are two camps: those that believe in warm/strict, and those that prefer softer, more restorative approaches. However, here lies a false dichotomy. You can practise warm/strict behaviour management, whilst also embracing restorative justice strategies.

The very label of the 'warm strict' approach shows us that, at the heart of it sits care and compassion: expecting the very best from pupils, showing them that we believe in them, providing aspirations, and showing that we really care for their future by accepting nothing but their absolute best behaviour and attitude.

Many of us will remember the classic advice, post initial teacher training, of 'never smile before Christmas'. However, this is a huge misconception: it is possible to be kind and strict; in fact, being strict *is* the kindness. As Doug Lemov says

> The fact is that the degree to which you are warm has no bearing on the degree to which you are strict...you should be caring, funny, warm, concerned, and nurturing – but also strict, by the book, relentless and sometimes inflexible.[1]

Being strict and being warm have to go hand in hand in order for our schools to be successful. We can make students smile and laugh, whilst holding them to account to create exceptional work, to contribute in the most scholarly manner. We can ask students how they are in the corridor, and take an interest in their personal lives when we know things are tough as well as issuing sanctions if we hear them using foul language, if their uniform isn't exceptionally presented. Our role as middle leaders is to encourage our staff to do all of the above.

We have to consider that all schools go about managing behaviour differently and we've yet to see a behaviour policy at one school mirrored exactly in that of

DOI: 10.4324/9781003160557-10

another. Some have a policy that is managed centrally by senior leadership, some have a more departmental-led approach, and some insist that teachers own the behaviour of their classes. We could debate for hours, days even, about which of these three approaches is the best, but what matters is that- at the heart of our behaviour management- we have the highest possible expectations of our pupils so that our teachers can use the finite time that they have in the classroom doing what they are there for: teaching quality lessons.

Teaching in a school where there are little to no consequences for behaviour is demoralising, frustrating and exhausting for classroom teachers, and it is the low-level disruptive behaviour that is the hardest to manage without clear, consistent sanctions specified within a behaviour policy. Below, a teacher gives their account of working in a school where low-level disruptive behaviour caused the most problems, but where the school did very little to combat it.

Case Study: C. Hutchinson, teacher of Humanities

I worked in a school whose behaviour policy was minimal, at best. I didn't realise during my time there just how much of a disadvantage this school was putting their students at, until I left. I was constantly told that the behaviour wasn't that bad, that it wasn't unsafe, that we should feel lucky to work with students whose worst traits are not putting their hand up and I figured that this made sense (at the time). Sanctions of any sort were on the teacher and it was assumed that, if a student was causing low-level disruption, that the fault lay with the class teacher. Of course, this resulted in a fear of reporting any sort of low-level disruption or requesting sanctions. To add to this, the use of card style reporting of behaviour issues meant that the teacher had to trek across a school and hand it to the relevant assistant head of year or head of year. Many colleagues suggested that, actually, this was a way to deter teachers from issuing sanctions or tracking poor behaviour which I rubbished at the time but now I see it.

I can honestly say that there were five classes a week that I dreaded, knowing that I would be constantly battling with low-level disruption, having to have restorative conversations with the culprits outside the door after sending them out, leaving the remaining 26+ class members without a teacher and interrupting their learning. I would go home constantly exhausted, would often feel incredibly undervalued as an expert in my subject who just spent most of his time firefighting in the classroom, constantly being interrupted. I didn't feel I was able to give the students my all because of this, and I think that the students that were impacted most negatively were those who did behave, those who did work hard and never interrupted. What's worse is that, despite this constant low-level disruption and how this left our most attentive students behind whilst we dealt with it, is that we were actively encouraged to reward those that usually misbehaved in order to 'keep them sweet'. The phrase 'kill them with kindness' was often used by SLT when being advised on how to deal with those students that constantly disrupted lessons. I can only imagine how this made the students who went above and beyond with their work ethic and attitude to learning feel.

I know of a time when a pregnant colleague told a class of 27 students that they were being too disruptive, and a number of students continued to ignore her requests for no shouting out, hands up, etc. When she raised this with her Head of Department and the students' head of year, the two middle leaders agreed that she was being 'over-emotional' with a heavy insinuation that this was down to the very obvious, heavily pregnant bump she was carrying. She went home crying, fed up with feeling constantly exhausted and ignored.

I eventually left this school where low-level disruption was accepted, even rewarded at times when the assistant headteacher in charge of behaviour invited disruptive students to his office for a 'catch up' with a cup of tea and a biscuit (no, this is not an exaggeration).

Since leaving this school, where I can honestly say that I don't know what the behaviour policy actually was, despite a number of INSET training days focusing on behaviour, I have worked in a number of schools with different approaches to behaviour. When I did leave, I realised just how much of my time low-level disruption was taking and how much it was truly wearing me down as a professional. Working in a school where there is a consistently clear behaviour policy and sanctions are centralised and managed by SLT is a breath of fresh air. I no longer have to spend my time extracting misbehaving students from the room, firefighting constant interruptions to my lessons. Instead, I can teach the subject that I adore and students can learn from me as the expert in the room. No longer do I have to spend my PPAs writing our sanction cards, and seeking out a Head of Year or Assistant Head of Year. Instead, I use them to plan lessons where I know I will be able to deliver quality-first teaching.

The sad thing is that the school without the behaviour policy on low-level disruption truly believes, still, that they have their students' best interests at heart with their approach to behaviour. I see on their social media about their rewards dinners, their reward trips and it's the same kids on them; the really, truly, well-behaved children are left behind. The constant low-level disruption breeds low expectations and does nothing to further their life chances. I just wish the SLT there would listen to the ones dealing with it every single lesson: their teachers. Until they do, they can't continue to claim that their school cares about its students like they pretend to do. I've seen it for myself, and until those students are held to consistently high expectations, they will sadly not achieve as well as they could.

As a middle leader, the weight of behaviour on your shoulders will vary greatly depending on the whole-school picture. Of course, the whole-school policy must be adhered to in order for there to be consistency in expectations, but you must also use the policy in a way that suits your team, your department/year team and your ethos. It's imperative that everybody in your team is singing from the same hymn sheet.

Behaviour management as a pastoral leader

As a pastoral leader, you will be responsible for the conduct of your year group/ key stage/house. It is your responsibility to create a culture for the students for whom you are responsible, in line with the whole-school policy. This culture must be so clear and walk so consistently implemented by members of your team that it translates into all contexts: lessons, breaktimes, walking to and from school – basically whenever that school uniform is on the students' backs.

However, in order to successfully embed such a culture, relationships are key. Your students have to know that you respect them in order for them to respect you back. You need to know each of your students to show that you truly care for them: learn their names, ask how their trial at whichever sports club they were trialling at went, issue behaviour sanction points when you hear them cursing in the corridor and tell them it's because you expected better, recommend a book you read that you think they might like, call them out on poor behaviour in lessons and say you want to see marked improvement.

Below is an account from a pastoral leader on what behaviour management means to them:

Case Study: Ed Gilchrist @gilchristeng) – English Teacher/Head of House

For me, behaviour management is the central focus of being a Head of Year: everything you do is geared towards getting young people to behave themselves in and out of the classroom. This ranges from daily "check ins" with key students to establishing and maintaining relationships with incredibly vulnerable young people in dire need of a positive adult role model. You need a big stick and an even bigger carrot to help support not just the young people but also colleagues in the classroom.

You need to be the young person's greatest ally and greatest fear; you need a direct hotline to home and don't be afraid to use it. You need to listen and make your office a safe space for them to sound off when necessary. You need to celebrate all their successes and pick them up when they fall.

Behaviour management as a curriculum leader

Regardless of what goes on outside of your department, your culture and ethos must be crystal clear across your department. Unsettled in MFL? Wet break? Row with a friend last lesson? None of this matters; they're in your subject now. Regardless of what goes on outside of those classrooms within your department, you make it clear that you have the highest of expectations, you want the very best out of each and every student and you want to use each expert on your team for what they're there to do: teach fantastic lessons where our students make fantastic progress.

In most good schools, the whole-school policy for behaviour is updated each academic year. When it is, sit with your team and work through it with them. Ask the questions: how will we implement this element of the policy? What doesn't quite work with our approach? What do we need to make clear in our own departmental policy that has been adapted? What is our rationale for doing so? If you ask one another these questions, and work together to understand the policy and how it works for you and your team, you give them ownership and reassure them of a united approach. Perhaps the whole-school policy covers it all, and you won't adapt it because there is no need, and it just works as it is. If that is the case, ensure that everybody feels the same and have the discussion about consistency in each classroom and the importance of rigidity in its use. **Enforce** it, **use** it, **support** it; no excuses.

By opening up behaviour as a dialogue, as part of department planning time, it puts out the flame of fear that so many have experienced. Make it clear that, as the curriculum leader, you will support them in following the policy as you have each agreed, in line whole with the whole-school outline. You'll find that, rather than worrying about how reporting of poor behaviour will be perceived in terms of their teaching, they will feel supported which will result in honesty and accuracy when it comes to the tracking of behaviour, attitude to learning and effort grade reporting, and that you'll have a more consistent picture to analyse and support the whole team with. Behaviour policies are there to make everybody's lives easier: ours, our team's, our students'. They are not there as a stick to judge teachers with and never, ever fall into the trap of thinking that poor behaviour is down to poor teaching as this is very rarely the case. Behaviour is a reflection of the culture that a school embeds and enforces. Make the culture in your department one where students feel empowered by high expectations, and confident through academic aspiration.

If you can get the culture of behaviour in your department right, then you will be absolutely astounded by the impact this has on your team's wellbeing. Eradicate low-level disruption in your classrooms through rigid enforcement, use, and support of the policy and your team will be energised, will feel valued and will enjoy their time at work far more than if low-level disruption continues to zap their time and energy.

There will be many of you reading this who, perhaps, don't feel supported by the whole- school behaviour policy in place at your school. When that whole-school approach is missing or inadequate then it's down to you as the curriculum leader to set up your own system with your team. Every single teacher in your department has to be reading the same script because consistency is absolutely key to any behaviour policy's success. This way, the sanctioning of behaviour becomes systemic and not personal and therefore relationships between students and their teachers are built on trust and respect.

Below are some practical strategies to implement within your department, in order to ensure that a behaviour policy is simple to follow and is successful without being onerous on you and your team.

Warn, move, remove

This is a strategy that many schools use, perhaps with different labels. This three-word strategy keeps it simple and needs little explaining. A student calls out or talks over you? Warn. They do it again? Move them. Again? Remove them either to an alternative classroom which you have prior agreed with your team, or to isolation (depending on your school's set up).

The students soon get used to the rigidity of this strategy and, whilst they might try to argue with you and therefore move straight from 'warn' to 'move', they will realise that you're serious and will – eventually – stop. As Tom Bennet says, 'The teacher must assert what the norms of the room should be, even if they fall short. Pupils must see and hear them promoted and required constantly'.[2]

If students don't comply and need to be removed, then it is usually down to the class teacher or pastoral team to communicate with parents and carers about the student's behaviour and next steps as well as ensuring that a conversation with the student is had (as soon as possible after the event), in order to nip this behaviour in the bud. If it becomes a continuous occurrence, then you should step in as the curriculum leader and be the one to contact home after three incidents of removal from the classroom in your subject.

Subject report

Subject reports support your classroom teachers to hone in on the insistence of high expectations within your subject, when students seem to be continuously disrupting lessons, putting in minimal effort and just not performing at the level that you expect within the culture of your department. It puts the responsibility for good behaviour on the student because they have to find the curriculum leader to whom they are reporting, and they have to ensure that the report is completed by their subject teacher.

Fresh start

It doesn't matter what happened in yesterday's lesson, because we don't hold grudges. Behaviour is not personal and every lesson is a fresh start to get it right this time. The student that continuously disrupted your lesson yesterday will be nervous about entering your classroom, but your smile as you greet them at the door just like every other student, is the 'warm' in warm/strict.

Routines

Routine is imperative for behaviour management and, whilst new routines will need time to become habits, they are key to a successful classroom. Every student must know exactly what to expect whenever they walk into your department regardless of which teacher they have. As a middle leader, you need to agree on the routines with your team and insist that they adhere to them with very little deviation. Perhaps you want all students to stand behind their desks at the start of the lesson until they are instructed to sit down by their teacher. Maybe you want every student to be reading silently for ten minutes at the start of the lesson. It is down to local context as to what these routines need to be, but for behaviour to be good then the students must know what to expect every single lesson.

Collective language

When discussing behaviour within your department, teachers should use 'in [subject] we...'. By doing so and using normative language, holds everybody (including teachers) to account in following the behaviour expectations. It also instills that warmth from warm/strict in that we are all one team. We are all in this together, and we will all work together in order to each be successful.

Taking time when taking the register

We have all been guilty of reeling off a list of names as fast as we can when we take a register so that it seems distant and impersonal: 'Jack? Here. Emily? Here...'. Stop, slow down. Speak to every single person in that room, with their name, and make eye contact. 'Good morning Jack. Morning Miss!', 'Good morning, Emily. Morning Miss!'. It shows them that you care and that harbours respect and trust and that's worth the extra two minutes it takes. And – very importantly – show your care and respect for students by pronouncing their names correctly; this can be tricky in the first lesson so address it upfront, apologise if necessary, and ask for clarity. Kaley was one of those students whose name was *never* pronounced correctly, but she distinctly remembers how much she appreciated the teachers that stopped during the register and asked me how to pronounce it accurately. We make a concerted effort now to make a note of the phonetic pronunciation in our seating plans and refer to it whenever we think we might get it wrong. Such a small act is such a huge deal with students.

Meet and greet

At the start of every lesson, teachers stand at the door and individually greet each student as they enter the room with a smile and a 'good afternoon' or relevant equivalent. Here, you can quietly address issues with uniform or signs of potential disruption before it even happens. Insist that non-uniform items are off before they cross the threshold of the classroom and do so every single lesson. Again, after a while, taking those items off before they reach the door becomes the norm and makes for a much more settled start to your department's lessons.

Keep it calm

It's imperative, as the adult professional in the room, that you and your team remain calm. It is rarely necessary to actually shout in a classroom and when we do so, it's a sure sign that we have lost control. Sure, a raised voice with a stern tone is sometimes required. But never ever should we need to yell *at* students.

With good behaviour management instilled at the core of your department, every single student can achieve. Factors about their socio-economic status, race, or other so-called challenges do not have to be the reason for students underachieving, they are simply obstacles which they can be trained to overcome with support and training through effective use of warm/strict behaviour management.

Leadership is key to improving behaviour standards because no teacher of any level or experience can intervene with behaviour at the same level as that of a middle or senior leader. As a middle leader, you are the model to your team of your departmental culture. Behaviour is as important as curriculum vision and the two should tie into your departmental ethos and, you must 'design, build and maintain'[3] the culture that you create. Think of behaviour management and culture as akin to that of your curriculum design. Your intention with each must be clear, and must be communicated effectively to both staff and students, and the implementation by every staff member involved must be consistent in order for students to learn effectively because 'it is the responsibility of every adult to help create in students the habit of self-restraint or self-regulation [and this] must be mastered before students can consider themselves to be truly free'.[4]

Case Study: A. Wilkes Secondary Curriculum Leader

Having interviewed for a more senior post than that of the one I was in at the time, I was successful in being offered the role. However, there was one tiny sticking point: I was moving from a completely whole-school approach to behaviour to one that was more diluted and put more of an onus on curriculum leads. There was no way I could turn down the opportunity to work at the school though: it was my perfect job, in the right location, and the interview day sold it to me for everything else. I decided that, if the whole-school approach wasn't as rigid as I needed it to be, that I would create a little microcosm in my own department.

I took the whole-school policy for behaviour, and essentially wrote it with more clarity for my department. Since coming into the role, and insisting that every teacher uses the same language for behaviour, the same sanctions, and has the same level of expectation for every single student, behaviour has improved ten-fold. It doesn't matter what happens in other areas of the school, at dinner or break time or in the lesson prior to mine. When students walk into our science labs, they know exactly what we expect of them. They're met at the door and greeted personally, they stand behind their desks until they're instructed to be seated by the teacher, and they're given three chances before they're asked to leave the room and work in isolation. Whilst I couldn't change the whole-school behaviour approach which would be the ideal, I proved that it worked within my subject and- as a result- the systems that I put in place are now being rolled out on a whole-school level to see the response.

Top tips for behaviour management

- Consistency is key.

- Show them that you care through high expectations.

- Make eye contact.

- Behaviour policies are implemented to support teaching staff, not to judge them against.

- Walk the walk as a middle leader, and be present.

Notes

1 Lemov, 2015.
2 https://tombennetttraining.co.uk/wp-content/uploads/2020/05/Tom_Bennett_summary.pdf
3 Bennet, Creating a Culture.
4 Bennet, Creating a Culture.

Bibliography

Bennett, Tom. (2016). "The Beginning Teacher's Behaviour Toolkit: a Summary." *Tom Bennett Training*, https://tombennetttraining.co.uk/wp-content/uploads/2020/05/Tom_Bennett_summary.pdf. Accessed 13 3 2021.

Bennett, Tom. (2017). *Creating a Culture: How School Leaders Can Optimise Behaviour*. Crown.

Lemov, Doug. (2010). *Teach Like a Champion 2.0*. Jossey-Bass Inc Pub.

10 CPD and coaching

As a middle leader, you have successfully completed at least some professional development in order to reach this level. But CPD doesn't stop. And, more importantly, you now need to support your team in theirs. One of our least favourite things to hear a teacher say is that they 'have their QTS', as if that means they have completed all the work they need to do in becoming a good teacher. We know that when we all got our QTS, we were nowhere near as good at teaching as we are now. Even just a few years ago, through lack of understanding of where and how to find really good CPD, we were pretty clueless about what made good teaching in many ways. This is not uncommon, and as a middle leader, you can be integral to changing that and helping your team progress their teaching and their careers.

> **Case Study: Ruth Daubney Teacher of Art**
>
> *I spent a long time at one school, not long after completing my training. My experience of CPD in this school was woeful, but having discussed this with many others, I know that it has been the norm for lots of us! The CPD I experienced consisted of the following:*
>
> *INSET Days and after school sessions – these usually involved some kind of SLT PowerPoint presentation that set up a task followed by group work, such as 'draw your ideal learner' on sugar paper; this was the epitome of discovery learning and, whilst I enjoyed having a chat with colleagues (and a whinge), we never really felt like we were learning anything new here. Sometimes external speakers would be brought in, which were more successful, but these were usually about specific PSHE areas rather than subject knowledge, or teaching and learning. In either case, what really was missing was any follow-up or evaluation. We did the activity or listened to the speaker, and that was ticked off. There wasn't any continuation to make sure whatever it was had been embedded which meant it was quickly forgotten about during the busy school term.*

On returning from the holidays, or staying late after a long day in the classroom, teachers really want to feel that they are doing something worthwhile. If what they are currently doing is thrown back at them, and they feel infantilized by childlike group work tasks, or they feel that the learning does not apply to them because it is too generic, they will not feel their time has been used well. And it is time that is our most precious commodity which means we must use it well. Moreover, teachers are our most important resource to invest in, so we should be maximising our input here and not wasting a moment.

Subject specificity

One thing that can make INSET time more focused is to make it more subject-specific, and this will be fantastic for you as a middle leader, as not only will you gain more control over the training, you will already have a better understanding of the needs within your team. If this is not something that has been done before in your school, when SLT are creating the calendar for the next academic year, perhaps you could approach them and ask for one or more of the following:

- An hourly session once a term, for example, to focus on subject knowledge development. This will work alongside your curriculum development, using your upcoming new units to inform the topics, or alongside your assessment, using your precise diagnostic data to identify common gaps.

- Sourcing of high-quality training through a range of different ways such as asking an external expert in that area. This would be beneficial in that you could give them specific criteria which they could tailor the session to, meaning that it was most useful for your team and context. However, this would definitely be the most costly option.

- Using something that has already been created; one of the best things that has come out of remote working is that there has been a plethora of recorded sessions from places like ResearchEd,[1] LitDrive,[2] TeachMeet Icons,[3] etc, from which you can find high-quality sessions that will likely have something suitable for your needs. Of course, there are also subject-specific societies, such as the National Geographic Society,[4] the Historical Association[5] and Massolit[6] who will have lectures and sessions available that can be used too.

- Finally, not all in-house CPD is bad CPD! You may have a member of your team who is an expert in an area that is really useful, or data shows that they teach a certain area really well; asking them to provide training for the rest of the team in this will be excellent CPD for the team, and also for them as it is an opportunity to develop their leadership experience.

Department time

We have already discussed in our chapter on Teaching and Learning how using departmental meeting time to model and embed new techniques gradually is a great idea. However, you may also want to have a larger focus on one area, for example, guided practice or modelling. In this case, it would be a good idea to have a larger session launching the idea, using a similar framework as suggested in the options above. Pedagogical CPD recordings can be found with ResearchEd, Myatt and Co[7], Sherrington[8], amongst others, and could provide you with exactly what you need if a specific visit or in-house session isn't an option. What is particularly important though is the follow-up to this. You will need to plan in when you will be using the elements of this pedagogy, when you will be evaluating and reviewing it, and when your team will be feeding back. If these steps are not completed, it will feel like there was no impetus, and it will be just another fad that gets forgotten about. And this is not what you want, because you will have chosen it carefully and thoughtfully because it is important for the team's development; also, if you are introducing something new to your team, you need to ensure that you are not overloading them and that you are giving lots of time for this one important thing to work. Teaching is busy and difficult, and takes up a lot of time and brain space! We need to focus on doing one thing well, so be highly selective and plan carefully before launching anything new with your team.

Case Study: Julia Allin Teacher of Biology

I have now sat down to many performance management meetings, or appraisals, or reviews. Whatever they may have been called, the process has been very similar, and I am sure it will sound familiar to some of you. You would conjure up three targets that you were going to achieve in that year to prove your worth and existence. One would probably be linked to results (even though the unions said we weren't supposed to do that); one would be linked to a wider school or pastoral issue or project; and one might involve you doing some planning or training for your department. Great. What a well-rounded professional you were proving yourself to be. And this was the next step: proof. Evidence was needed, meaning one of these targets needed to be linked to a lesson observation. If you were really organised, you would get your timetables out there and then, find the suitable lesson, write this into your planner and highlight it. Even the most disorganised teachers would ensure that they had at least chosen the right class – the best class. Compliant, eager to please, just knowledgeable enough to make you look good, but so you could still make sure you showed progress. And when that lesson observation came, come hell or high water, regardless of what you were really teaching you could pull out your failsafe 'good with outstanding features' showpiece that ran like clockwork and would get you what you needed: proof that you were not a bad teacher. Job ticked off for another year. Phew! What a nonsense. I soon found that, regardless of the lesson I taught, I ended up with the same lesson grading. I also found that I often got feedback for my lesson that didn't match up to what happened in the classroom, and when I brought it up, the observer happily changed it, which showed me that they hadn't even really been paying attention! This isn't really surprising when they were watching the same show lessons on repeat though, I suppose! So, the grading seemed pointless - what is the actual benefit of grading anyway? And the feedback seemed pointless too! In the end,

I stopped caring about observations. I stopped putting on a show. I stopped picking a class that I thought would be great to watch. I told them to come along to whatever they wanted and I just taught whatever I happened to be teaching. And, do you know what? My grading didn't actually change (partly because I don't think anyone really understood grading anyway and it is so subjective!). But my feedback did because it was actually more useful and I cared more about it as it was reflecting my real teaching. The only problem that I found was that the observers, not having much experience in the reality of lessons, weren't very adept in helping to improve the areas of development, and this left me wondering how on earth I could get better and feeling annoyed and frustrated about the system across the department and school.

Developmental feedback

Once your team has a foundation of core techniques (see the chapter on Teaching and Learning), you can start to think about a more individualised approach to developing teaching and learning that will form part of your observation cycle. Is the observation style in the case study above really the best thing for development as a teacher? No. And it's not designed to be. It is judgement dressed up as development; this does not improve teaching and learning.

With this possibly being your one observation in a whole term or even year, one would imagine that the feedback would be something of great value and carefully honed. Unfortunately, this has regularly not been the case. When we were researching this book we asked the teachers of Twitter about their experiences of observation feedback, and we received myriad stories of terrible feedback that were either completely unactionable with vague comments about missing 'the thing', completely arbitrary such as to do with room temperature, or even detrimental to learning for the sake of ticking a box, such as specific timings allowed for teacher explanation and questioning (sometimes known as *teacher talk...*). And most of the examples we were told started with, *I didn't get graded Outstanding because...*

This is the problem with a model that is trying to be both summative and formative: just like a child doing a mock exam, the focus is always on the grade, and not on the feedback. The feedback, which should be paramount, becomes the afterthought: another box to tick rather than a systematic action which, when focused on, will move you towards making you a better practitioner. In these cases, the feedback still came after the grade in the mind of the teachers, and the lack of quality in the examples of feedback shows us that it probably was an afterthought for the observer too.

Coaching

Some of the most effective CPD, and the most personal, is coaching. What you need to become is a coach, or use coaches to develop teaching and learning in your team. Your view of coaching may be more aligned with what we would probably term 'growth' coaching, or basic coaching, where a coach works collaboratively in a guidance role, mainly through asking questions to enable the person being coached to self-direct their development, and come up with their own answers. We know a lot of people view this very positively, but for many, it can actually be frustrating. We think that is especially true of our Early Career Teachers, or indeed more experienced teachers with whom we are trying to develop new strategies or ways of working which will feel alien and uncertain. Instructional Coaching is different because it is expert-led and more directive. Instructional coaches need to be chosen carefully as they need to be able to embody the pedagogy they are developing in the teachers so that they can help them to develop in that.

Instructional coaching

As this reference from a research paper from Dr Lorraine Hammond summarises:

> Instructional coaches have a strong pedagogical knowledge and content expertise in the area they coach: a specialist who has distinct expertise in the discrete field in which they coach. They work with teachers to improve their practice by modelling, co-planning and co-teaching, as well as observing and providing feedback.[9]

So, with instructional coaching, the focus is less 'personal', and more focused on improving outcomes for our learners. Improving teacher instruction is vital for this. Studies have shown the vast difference that the quality of teacher instruction has on learning, such as a study by Hanushek and Rivken[10] which showed that in a group of 50 teachers, the most effective could teach the same learning in six months that the least effective taught in two years. And several studies[11] have shown that it is those learners who come from disadvantaged backgrounds who benefit the most, so through improving teacher instruction, we are literally changing and bettering lives.

Putting instructional coaching into action requires setting up the coaching relationships. What is really important here is that there is a strong level of trust between you. This works on different levels. Firstly, there needs to be a common understanding that this is about development and not judgement. As a line manager, you may not be the best person to be a teacher's coach, particularly if they are a more experienced teacher, who is more likely to be concerned that this 'coaching' is somehow trying to catch them out, so you may need to think about who is a better person to coach. If you have a Lead Practitioner, this may be the perfect role for that person. There also needs to be clarity around communication. Is the coach to share feedback with anyone? That needs to be made clear, as otherwise, developmental feedback could be wrongly used to make judgements. There also needs to be a level of trust in the coach as the expert. We know that if we were training for a marathon, we would want someone like Paula Radcliffe to be coaching us and that we would trust in them to know what they were doing because that is their area of expertise.

A lot of this could come from a whole-school culture, but if not, you will need to work hard to develop a departmental culture, and that may take some time; it is important that coaching is not seen as something just for the 'struggling' teachers. Enthusiastic and vocal teachers proliferating about their coaching journey, including those who are in leadership positions, can help to build a culture that shows that we are all in this together – for the sake of the children, and not for ourselves – ensure that you are taking part in the coaching process too. We need to build the confidence to trust a coach to come and see that tricky, frustrating and irksome lesson that we are really struggling with, so that they can help us to get that better with them, rather than just showing off our obedient cleverclogs class.

Observations

Once the coaching partnership is established, observations can begin. But these are not like the observations of some of those performance management experiences we saw in the case study. Firstly, they are very regular, which means you can achieve visible, incremental improvement. It also means the observations become less of an event. This is not putting on a show – it is seeing what your normal everyday teaching looks like. What is the point of being an 'Outstanding' teacher two or three times a year? Schools want and students need consistently effective teachers.

Secondly, observations can be short. 15 to 20 minutes is enough time to see what needs to be improved here. And that means that you can coach more than one teacher more easily, fitting in two or three observations in a lesson, meaning more and faster improvement for your department. This is because the observations are focused. If you are using Paul Bambrick-Santoyo's model, from *Get Better Faster*[12] or *Leverage Leadership,*[13] you may follow what is called a 'waterfall' approach. This means that you work from the top of a list of criteria which need to be established and mastered first and work down. As soon as you identify an action point that isn't being met, you can leave that lesson, because that is the one thing you are going to work on this week.

Alternatively, you might want to identify the highest leverage point in that lesson – the one thing that you saw that will make the most difference to that teacher and their learners, then that will be the one thing you focus on that week. For example, if you had to choose between focussing on stretching questioning or establishing a calm and focused entry to the lesson, the highest leverage is the entry to the lesson and therefore is the one you would focus your feedback and coaching conversation on.

Setting targets

If you are already moving along your coaching journey, you will have a focus identified from the previous week that you will be looking out for to see if they have embedded it into their practice.

Selecting your action step is absolutely critical. It needs to be purposeful, very specific and achievable within a week. The purpose will come from your shared goal and understanding of what 'good' looks like from your deliberate practice, and the shared language that comes with this; it needs to be something that will make the teaching better, something that can be genericised to apply to the majority of their lessons. Precision is also extremely important when deciding action steps, a word used in *Get Better Faster* is granular[14] – like grains of sand. Picking out that fine detail that can be refined and made perfect.

And finally, actionable. This needs to be something that can be achieved within the coming week – we are looking at swift, but sustained improvement, building up brilliant practice step by step as each of these is mastered.

The coaching session

At last, we get onto the most important part of the process: the coaching session itself. It will be imperative to have protected time for this, a place where the coach and teacher won't be disturbed, and with enough time to act on the feedback; this poses a challenge for you as the middle leader. How will you secure this time? If your school does not use this model en masse, can this form part of directed time for your department in lieu of some other engagement? Could you ask to be a pilot of this approach? Also, the coach cannot just waltz into this feedback session without prior thought – it needs preparation and scripting. In fact, as time is so precious, you may want to assign clear timings to each section of this session. This is something that Dixons Academies do, and we recommend watching Dixons OpenSource for their model of this if you desire that level of clarity and control, which ensures efficiency and effectiveness.[15]

Like/notice/wonder

One useful idea is the like/ notice/ wonder framework. Starting with the positives: what you liked. But no empty platitudes here –this kind of praise is not effective (for more about giving candid feedback see the chapter on difficult conversations). The positive feedback needs to give a clear example and also why this was effective. For example, rather than: *I loved the start of your lesson!* It would be better to say: *I liked how your use of clear instructions for the do now activity meant you had a calm and focused start to the lesson, and meant everyone engaged with the retrieval activity.*

Now, you need to get onto that action point. You say what you 'noticed' (the problem), and then what you 'wonder' (the solution). And, just like we think carefully about the order of our wording in the classroom (see Adam Boxer on 'front loading' instructions[16]), it is a good idea to 'front load' your action step with *why*, the purpose. So rather than: *Use a clear visual cue at the end of the activity*, you could say: *I noticed that not all of the class were listening to the feedback on the retrieval exercise. So that you are sure that everyone is focused on you, I wonder if a clear visual cue would help.*

Modelling

The next steps are vital: more modelling and deliberate practice. This again needs to be scripted, and performed as if you are in front of the class. For the action step, you should share the success criteria: for example, a clear and confident voice and stance, a repeated visual cue so the class knows what to expect, brevity of language, to be seen looking and, use non-verbal signals to prompt compliance. You would now stand up and deliver this pre-scripted example of this action step. Then the teacher can explain how you met those criteria in your model. Together you would then identify a similar moment in their lessons, and script the routine they want to practise.

Next comes the deliberate practice – the teacher needs to stand up and deliver their script in just the same way. Afterwards, the coach uses the success criteria to evaluate. Then they practise again, correcting anything that didn't go well. The important thing here is that the deliberate practice element needs to continue beyond the point where they get their script perfect; they need to embed the 'right way' of doing it. And as they get better, this means that you can start to increase the complexity – what if Tom doesn't put his pen down? What if Fatimah starts talking? What if somebody walks in late? The more times the teacher can practise this in a safe space with you, the closer they get to automaticity, which means getting it right when it really matters: in their lessons. It's important to keep practising beyond perfection because practice makes permanent. The version we want to be permanent is the (almost) perfect one!

Finally, you can co-plan exactly when this action step will be used in lessons that week, and look forward to seeing it in action in your next observation. This process then continues, so you have a cyclical model of observation, setting of action steps, deliberate practice and observation again.

Conclusion

The purpose of CPD is to develop your team as a whole, as well as each individual member, and by using the strategies above you can ensure that your department and school can flourish, whilst your individual team members feel fulfilled, valued, and motivated in their work. It also means that if and when you are promoted, you can be confident that you have fantastic people waiting to step into your middle leader shoes!

Top tips for CPD and coaching

- Make sure that CPD sessions are tailored to your subject.

- Make sure that CPD sessions are tailored to the individuals and the context.

- Don't overload – select carefully and give it time to embed.

- Evaluate repeatedly so that you can be sure that the training is having an effect.

- Use instructional coaching instead of formal graded lesson observations.

Notes

1 https://researched.org.uk/category/researched-home/
2 https://litdrive.org.uk/remotecpd
3 https://www.teachmeeticons.com/event-recordings
4 https://www.nationalgeographic.org/education/professional-development/
5 https://www.history.org.uk/secondary/categories/cpd
6 https://www.massolit.io/
7 https://myattandco.com/
8 https://teacherhead.com/youtube/
9 Hammond, L., & Moore, W. M. (2018). Teachers Taking up Explicit Instruction: The Impact of a Professional Development and Directive Instructional Coaching Model. Australian Journal of Teacher Education, 43(7).
10 Hanushek, Eric & Rivkin, Steven. (2006). Chapter 18 Teacher Quality. Handbook of the Economics of Education. 2. 1051–1078. 10.1016/S1574-0692(06)02018-6.
11 See: Wiliam, D. (2016) Leadership for Teacher Learning West Palm Beach, FL: Learning Sciences International; Timperley, Helen & Wilson, Aaron & Barrar, Heather & Fung, Irene & Education, New. (2007). Professional learning and development: a best evidence synthesis iteration. http://lst-iiep.iiep-unesco.org/cgi-bin/wwwi32.exe/[in=epidoc1. in]/?t2000=025049/(100); and Hamre, B. K., & Pianta, R. C. (2005). Can Instructional and Emotional Support in the First-Grade Classroom Make a Difference for Children at Risk of School Failure? Child Development, 76, 949–967. http://dx.doi.org/10.1111/j. 1467-8624.2005.00889.x
12 Bambrick-Santoyo, P. (2016). *Get better faster: A 90-day plan for coaching new teachers.* John Wiley & Sons.
13 BAMBRICH-SANTOYO, P. (2018) *Leverage Leadership 2.0*: A Practical Guide to Building Exceptional Schools. San Francisco: Jossey-Bass.
14 Ibid.
15 Dixons OpenSource. (2020). *Coaching.* [video] Available at: https://www.youtube.com/watch?v=wrm0d4VjLNw [Accessed 18 May 2021].
16 Boxer, A. (2020). *Front-loading.* [online] A Chemical Orthodoxy. Available at: https://achemicalorthodoxy.wordpress.com/2020/10/14/front-loading/ [Accessed 27 August 2021].

Bibliography

Bambrick-Santoyo, P. (2016). *Get better faster: A 90-day plan for coaching new teachers.* John Wiley & Sons.

Bambrich-Santoyo, P. (2018). *Leverage Leadership 2.0*: A Practical Guide to Building Exceptional Schools. San Francisco: Jossey-Bass.

Boxer, A. (2020). *Front-loading.* [online] A Chemical Orthodoxy. Available at: https://achemicalorthodoxy.wordpress.com/2020/10/14/front-loading/ [Accessed 27 August 2021].

Dixons OpenSource (2020). *Coaching.* [video] Available at: https://www.youtube.com/watch?v=wrm0d4VjLNw [Accessed 18 May 2021].

Hammond, L., & Moore, W. M. (2018). "Teachers Taking up Explicit Instruction: The Impact of a Professional Development and Directive Instructional Coaching Model". *Australian Journal of Teacher Education, 43*(7), 115.

Hamre, B. K., & Pianta, R. C. (2005). "Can Instructional and Emotional Support in the First-Grade Classroom Make a Difference for Children at Risk of School Failure?" *Child Development*, 76, 949–967. 10.1111/j.1467-8624.2005.00889.x

Hanushek, Eric & Rivkin, Steven. (2006). "Chapter 18 Teacher Quality". *Handbook of the Economics of Education*, 2, 1051–1078. 10.1016/S1574-0692(06)02018-6.

Timperley, Helen, Wilson, Aaron, Barrar, Heather, Fung, Irene & Education, New. (2007). Professional learning and development: a best evidence synthesis iteration. http://lst-iiep.iiep-unesco.org/cgi-bin/wwwi32.exe/[in=epidoc1.in]/?t2000=025049/(100)

Wiliam, D. (2016). *Leadership for Teacher Learning West Palm Beach*, FL: Learning Sciences International.

11 Social media

Social media has become a hive of teacher minds buzzing with CPD opportunities, professional discourse and resources in abundance. Many teachers use platforms such as Twitter, WeAreinBeta and Facebook as places to network, to learn from one another, and to access CPD as and when they wish.

The uptake in engagement on such platforms is a sign of the times and, for the most part, a positive step in the right direction towards self-sought training, cost-effective networking and tailored CPD. However, using a public social media account doesn't come without some risk, and it's important that as middle leaders we support our team to use social media positively, if they choose to use it in the first place, and that we use our position to influence school views and policies on social media usage.

It's really important to mention that we should never expect our team members to use social media if they're not comfortable doing so; we should never judge them for not wanting to engage via social media, outside of working hours, for the purpose of work. What we do as educators in our own time is entirely up to us; whilst many of us enjoy professional discourse outside of work, many don't and neither preference makes us a better or worse teacher or leader.

In the last five years or so, social media has become a much more utilised resource by those of us in education, particularly Twitter or 'edutwitter' as it is commonly known. It is here we can 'meet' a range of colleagues nationwide, where we can find some of the most informative blogs, and where affordable, remote CPD is available in abundance. We are *finally* able to wave goodbye to the days of CPD sessions that cost an absolute fortune but where we learnt very little, that were full of time-wasting gimmicks, and that were not focussed to the needs of us as individuals or as wider teams, but on a whole-school level just to fill INSET time. Dare I say that passive learning for teachers on INSET is becoming a thing of the past?

With funding cuts sadly impacting the opportunity to be able to attend training courses where we met new people, shared resources and enjoyed a free lunch (the best bit?), we have to accept that remote, online CPD that is tailored to our developmental needs is not only often more convenient, but also a way of saving money in times where finances are tight. So it's time to embrace the more informal peer-to-peer learning promoted through the likes of Twitter such as ResearchEd, WomenEd, LitDrive, Myatt & Co and BrewEd events.

Of course, as with anything, there are positive and negative elements to using social media as a form of continued professional development, but we believe that the positive elements considerably outweigh the negative. However, we would be hypocrites if we didn't admit that there are corners of the internet as a whole – with social media in its very own corner – that we must be acutely aware of and that we must support our teams in understanding fully:

- Having a profile on Twitter or any other social media platform that is 'public' means that anybody from the public can see your tweets and communicate with you. Parents and pupils may wish to try and get in touch with you, and this is a very difficult situation to be put in. Many teachers do choose to keep a public profile in order to be able to better engage with the wider collegiate network and that's fine, but be sure to avoid 1-1 communication with parents and pupils in order to safeguard yourself.

- Sadly, when people 'hide' behind a keyboard, they can interact in ways that they never would in a working environment. Not everybody that you engage with via social media will be inspirational, generous and well-meaning. Trolls exist as much on professional social media platforms as they do on personal ones and it's so important that we utilise the mute and block options available to us on said platforms in order to not become bombarded with unpleasantries and keyboard warriors.

- Very rarely, you may become a victim to professional sabotage. This links to the point I make later about awareness of the impression of our online footprint. Once we say something online, particularly in a public domain, it can be interpreted entirely differently from how we intended. Even when deleted, it can be screenshot and sent to employers or seniors and can be framed in a way that misrepresents you and your professional intentions, and replies to the tweet/status/upload can still be read and misinterpretations spread like wildfire.

- Social media is addictive. We teach our children this all the time, and we often reassure them that the internet isn't real life. A professional social media account can easily draw you back to your phone or electronic device, even when wanting to 'switch off'. If you want to use social media professionally, it's incredibly important that you don't allow it to consume you and that you sustain a positive work/life balance.

- It's very easy to feel inadequate as a result of social media because there are a select number of educators who just keep giving exceptionally. This doesn't mean that you have to match up to this and put pressure on yourself to do the same. Everybody's life is different, and social media is only ever a snapshot of a whole picture.

■ At times, social media can feel 'cliquey' and this in itself can feel really quite isolating as somebody who, perhaps, isn't in one of those 'cliques'. Remember that a number of the people you're likely to follow will have met in real life either as real-life colleagues or at 'educonferences'. Don't worry if you don't fit in a clique, and certainly don't allow such groups of people to make you feel uncomfortable for being on a social media platform that is open to all. Often, social media platforms can feel like the school playground where there are certain groups of people out to criticise others. Always be mindful that we are all one team; there is no need for competition. Empowered people, empower others. If they're not empowering you, and only out for self-gain, then they're not worthy of your energy.

■ There is also an expectation of those that engage on 'edutwitter' to follow an unofficial 'etiquette' such as:

- avoiding the perceived passive-aggression of subtweeting or 'vague-booking' (the social media equivalent of talking about somebody behind their back).

- ensuring that you follow with intent, not just to increase your own follower count. If you follow thousands of people just because you want them to follow you back, you'll find that there is an abundance of irrelevant information on your feed and this defeats the very object of tailoring your CPD.

- when referencing somebody else's work, always credit them.

- remembering that social media is seen as a community and, rather than taking everything from it, you should contribute and provide value to others as they do for you.

- Respecting the use of the block and mute button, particularly on Twitter. People may block you, and Twitter enjoys telling you that – unlike Facebook which simply pretends that the one who did the blocking doesn't exist. Don't let it get to you personally; we all have a right to block, mute and unfollow whomsoever we wish to.

- Above all: thinking about what you post, just like we tell children: is it kind? Is it relevant? Is it true? Is it necessary?

Case Study: G Parker, Secondary School Head of Year

I tweeted about teaching students about the concept of racism and I was truly unprepared for the flood of abuse that was unleashed after a right-wing activist group flagged me as a 'danger to children'. I had been called a 'child abuser', a 'neonazi' and accused of 'indoctrinating' children.

I use Twitter regularly to share ideas, write blogs and partake in professional discourse. Many of the stances that I take are, perhaps, controversial but I had – until this point – only ever experienced professional debate and discourse that was respectful and pleasant. This time was different; this was an attack on my professional integrity. It was so bad that I had to not just uninstall the app but deactivate my profile altogether. I couldn't help but feel that people were deliberately attempting to tarnish my professional reputation; something that I had worked so hard on over 17 years in education. It really affected my mental wellbeing, and left me physically unwell. My initial tweet was intended to be a learning point for me, in order to answer questions posed to me by my students. Instead of seeing me for the conscientious teacher that I am, I was attacked and accused of brainwashing the students whom I care so much for. Complaints were made to my school about the content of my tweet, and I was formally investigated. Of course, nothing came of it, but it was an extremely difficult time in my life and career and one which I wouldn't wish on my worst enemy. All because I wanted to be able to adequately provide a broad array of resources and theories to answer a question posed to me by a curious student in my class.

I have, since, rejoined Twitter. However, I approach it with much more caution. Fear even. I find myself asking 'am I going to be piled on for this?' and the anxiety that comes with asking questions that contain controversial content is too much for me to bear sometimes.

Getting started with a professional social media account

It's important, if we decide to engage on social media in a professional capacity, that we adhere to the same rules that we would as if meeting people at work in person for the first time, and that we always consider the safeguarding of our students when we post about anything involving them. We must be mindful that, if our profile is public, parents and students may well be privy to our discourse, and we must always be very sure that we understand our place of work's social media policy. Anything that you say can come back to you, and if it has the potential to cause disrepute for where you work then you could be in some serious trouble, and that could impact your career forever. Just as we tell our students the importance of keeping themselves safe online, we must do the same. The best advice? Interact with people that you know in real life at first; sit back and observe how people interact, and stop and ask if you would say what you're about to post online, in real life at work? If not then don't post it. By sitting back and observing then you can understand the platform you are using and learn from others the best way to interact via a keyboard with your collegiate network. There are a number of trusted organisations and individuals on Twitter that can be followed as 'model accounts'.

As a middle leader, if members of your team are wanting to engage via social media platforms for professional purposes, then it would be the right thing to do to provide them with a list of trusted organisations and accounts, as well as being the one in your team to model the effective use of social media.

Follow specific tags relevant to your field

There are a range of different chats defined via hashtags on Twitter that we can follow as professionals, either to observe or engage in professional discourse. For example #SLTchat, #MLTchat, #EngChat. These hashtags allow for the discourse to be found easily even in retrospect, and the discourse acts as an online staffroom where teachers from a diverse array of contexts offer their perspective on some of the most pressing topics in education at the time.

Additionally, on Facebook there are various groups for educators, from department-specific forums to those for teaching specific exam board courses. They are usually supportive and helpful places where you can ask for support from like-minded colleagues. Do remember though, that these are usually public, so remember not to say anything that could be interpreted as bringing your school into disrepute.

Be true to your professional self, even behind the keyboard

As educators, we are passionate about what we do and we can find ourselves getting drawn into conversations where we often disagree with one of our colleagues. This happens online too and it's so important to remember that – despite our passions – we must remain professional at all times. Just as keyboard warriors and trolls exist on personal social media accounts, they do so in the professional world of social media too and it is a commonly mentioned factor that #edutwitter (particularly in the holidays) can be argumentative and toxic at times. Remember that everything you post on social media should be something that you would be willing to say to a person's face during a professional meeting. If your account is one that you engage with professionally, then the persona that you present through it must also be your professional self. Being behind a keyboard doesn't negate the professional standards required to be privileged enough to work in education, and if you feel that discussions are becoming heated and unprofessional then be the bigger person and walk away from the conversation, just as you would at work if somebody was hurling insults at you, or raising their voice in a debate; you don't deserve to spoken to like that and you definitely don't need to get involved in a back-and-forth on a public platform where you may be watched by your colleagues, your students, or the local community. Model how you wish to be treated by others, in the way that you engage with them. Maintain professionalism, respect and politeness in your posts and never resort to debating about people; always stick with concepts and ideas.

Balancing the profession with personal

Whether you share information about your personal life via your professional account or not is entirely up to you. If you write a blog, for example, and you think that knowing you is a part of that, then it makes sense to present yourself personally as well as professionally, but sharing anything too revealing about yourself on a public platform in which you declare you are a teacher is perhaps not the best idea. If you're an advocate for flexible working then perhaps sharing things about your family, lifestyle and why that's important is something that helps you with that advocacy. Equally, if you're passionate about something then it's likely you'll share your personal opinion.

Just like when we are in the classroom, it's okay to present yourself as a real person. You're not just a teaching robot who goes in the cupboard at the end of the day; you are a human being, somebody's parent, somebody's child, somebody's sibling, somebody's wife/husband/partner/friend. It's about knowing the balance of what to share. All three of us who are writing this book share elements of our personal lives: pictures of our children, when we have seen fellow 'edutweeters' for meals/drinks, and moments of personal accomplishment. Yes, we are teachers and leaders, but it's important that people see us as real people. Just as the last paragraph explained, being true to your professional self is paramount here. Below is a case study of somebody who was reprimanded for sharing personal information on Twitter, despite doing so due to their beliefs in the need to remove the stigma surrounding mental health.

Case Study: J. Hughes, Teacher of MFL

I'd been using Twitter for some time, and had also begun to write a blog about my experiences of teaching and learning as my following grew. It was incredibly important for me that the people who engaged with my professional Twitter profile and who read my blog knew me personally in order to relate to the things that I was writing: I am a father, a brother and a long-term sufferer of General Anxiety Disorder. The latter is something that I have, perhaps more recently, been really quite open about. Too many young men are afraid to talk about their mental health openly, and the statistics for male suicide as a result are simply heartbreaking. I decided that it was almost a moral obligation, with a following of thousands, to speak openly about my experience with mental health. Of course, I never went into too much personal detail. I did, however, write blogs and tweets about my mental breakdown due to burnt out in 2017. I did openly discuss my need for regular therapy and medication in order to control my mental health and maintain my wellness. All of these things, as well as the resources that I shared, were a huge part of who I was as a teacher. I taught kids who I could see didn't feel comfortable discussing their emotions and I figured that – by seeing somebody as 'successful' as I was discussing mental health struggles as part of life – it might support them to feel more comfortable to talk about their own. Never once did I tweet about my mental health in an attempt to gain sympathy or likes, and I certainly didn't 'overshare' as I was once told by my line manager.

After writing a really quite personal blog about my experience with burnout and the need for self-care one Saturday, I was called into my line manager's office on the Monday morning. A printed copy of my blog was placed on a desk in front of me and I was asked why I thought it was appropriate to share such 'personal information on such a public platform'. I tried, in vain, to explain that the intention behind that blog was to support others to stop being ashamed of their own mental health issues, that I was advocating for the removal of a stigma that has – for too long – been associated with mental health.

I was told that I was 'oversharing' and that it was 'against the Teaching Standards'; that I should 'be mindful of the fact that parents and students had access to this very public blog piece'.

I took on board what I was told by my line manager, but I also explained that this wasn't me oversharing; that actually I had shared very little about the breakdown details. I explained that the very fact that I was being pulled in for a conversation about a blog I wrote, with the intention of removing a damaging stigma surrounding mental health, being 'too personal' highlighted the very need for something so honest to be in the public domain. I listened to my line manager, and I spoke to my union. I later explained to my line manager that my blog would continue to be an honest account of my teaching and learning, a place for nationwide colleagues to take free resources, but also a place where I would shout from the rooftops about the need to remove the stigma surrounding mental health. We agreed that I should continue, but that I was to be mindful about personal details shared which goes without saying. There are some things about a teacher or colleague that others don't need to know, but there are some things that – in a position of power and authority that we are so privileged to have – we must advocate for. Mental health allyship was mine.

Imposter syndrome

We hear things all the time about the way people portray themselves on social media isn't always the truest reflection of them, but the idealistic one. The same applies to teachers on social media. Whilst there are a number of educators who are so beautifully honest and will admit when they have had a bad day, there are others who are seemingly perfect. Social media never paints the full picture and it's far too easy to draw comparisons with an idealistic presentation on Twitter/Facebook/Instagram with yourself. We are often our own worst enemies, but it's so important to remember that everybody works in different ways, has different priorities, and therefore we cannot be compared. Teaching and middle leadership can be hard enough without allowing social media and imposter syndrome to make us feel inadequate.

There is also a range of educators on social media whose voices seem to be everywhere. This can feel quite isolating at times as they seem to dominate timelines, CPD events, and this concept of 'edulebrities' is daunting and damaging. In order to use social media whilst being able to sustain sanity, this putting people up on a pedestal has to stop. Nobody is perfect, and if a social media account tells you otherwise then reassure yourself that it is *probably* (definitely) not a true representation of the whole picture.

It's very easy to feel overwhelmed from the barrage of ideas that can be presented to you from scrolling through a teacher feed, be that on Twitter, Facebook, or any other platform. This barrage of different ideas can often feel impossible to even get started with, and it can cause you to doubt yourself. But don't let it. We are not built to run with hundreds of ideas at once, and even if we were then those ideas and implementation of initiatives would fizzle out and serve very little purpose. Instead of trying to take on board every single good idea that you've read on social media, allow yourself time to prioritise ones that you think would be useful. If somebody put 24 books about teaching in front of you on a desk, you wouldn't be able to read them all at once nor implement the ideas that they present within them. Don't chastise yourself for being a human and not a machine!

Likes, retweets and followers do not determine your worth

I realise that I'm getting to the point in this chapter where I sound like I'm delivering an internet safety PSHE lesson, but these points are important! Social media is addictive, and the affirmation that comes with likes/comments/retweets or posts and an increasing number of followers can be falsely reassuring. If you find yourself checking how many likes a post has got, or how many followers you've gained that day, then you're losing track of the very purpose you chose to use social media for professional purposes. Yes, it's exciting when you start to gather a lot of followers, or if you've had hundreds of likes on a post you've written. But know one thing: the more engagement you gain on social media platforms, means the more open you are to trolls and abusive responses to said tweets. Do not allow yourself to be drawn into the false promise of retweets, likes or followers. If you're true to yourself and your ethos as an educator or leader, then it doesn't matter if you have ten thousand followers or three followers. What matters is that you're using the platform to develop, discuss and debate professionally in order to be a better teacher to the students whose lives you are changing.

What is the role of the Middle Leader, when it comes to professional social media use?

Slowly, Slowly...

For a team who are not familiar with the likes of Twitter, Facebook teaching groups, or the other platforms available, bombarding people with ideas that you've seen on said platforms can be overwhelming. Whilst you may be well-versed in the use of social media, your team may not. Don't speak to your team about so and so 'from Twitter' as if they're expected to know them or the platform. As soon as you make them feel out of the loop, you'll find they switch off. It's remarkable how similar we are to students, really, isn't it?

Just as when we attend in-person CPD courses, we can't just bring an idea in the next day and expect everybody to implement it in the classroom that day. It takes time to bring an idea to the table, to discuss it within the context that you work in, and to see how others react to it. By all means, bring inspiration from social media discussions, and blogs, to departmental meetings but don't be that leader that goes 'I read this on Twitter and think it's a great idea, we need to do it'. You have to contextualise the concepts, support and guide your team in understanding the intent, how it should be implemented, and what the impact is likely to be. It's so important to remember that, just because somebody with a large following tweeted something, it doesn't mean that it works everywhere, regardless of likes and retweets!

Taking the resources

We are a truly generous profession, and that's just wonderful. There are educators out there who share resources, for free, in abundance: @spryke, @funkypedagogy, @_codexterous and @mathew_lynch44, @katejones_teach, @mrbartonmaths to name a few. This generosity saves time and workload for all of us and it's so important that we take on this generous offer of resources. It's also important, however, to know that we cannot just pick up a resource from a completely different context just because it is on Twitter, and expect it to work as is in our own contexts. Most of the time, small tweaks are necessary to ensure that it is fit for our context. Present your teams with resources from social media, by all means, but don't expect them to pick it up and run with it. Spend time co-planning how to use it, adapting it to suit the local needs of your cohorts, and tweaking it so that it works alongside your curriculum.

Just as there is etiquette to follow when engaging on social media, it is also common courtesy to acknowledge the original maker of a resource that you are using. There have been instances when people have attended a paid course and, when useful resources have been handed out, the attendees have recognised them as their own. Whilst those that share resources are pleased to help others out, it can be frustrating when somebody tries to pass them off as their own work.

Modelling

As leaders, we are expected to show our team members *how* something is done well. The same concept applies with social media. Ask yourself this question: online, am I who I would want my team members to be? It's really easy to get dragged into the negativity that often infiltrates social media feeds but **nobody** needs to read that their leader has sat behind a keyboard and moaned all evening after a bad day. If you are criticising, then you must be constructive in doing so, just as you would in the real-life workplace. Be mindful of the language that you utilise, the people whom you identify, and the fact that – once something is posted online – it remains a permanent impression of your online footprint.

Similarly, the amount of time that you spend on CPD via online social media platforms such as engaging with @ChatMLT, @SLTchat, etc, needs to be one that models a healthy work/life balance. Our lives and flexibility range, of course, but the NQT who looks up to you as their Head of Department or Head of Year needs to know that it isn't expected of them to spend hours after school engaging in professional discourse and that it is okay to switch off.

Using social media on behalf of your department or year team

Most schools have their very own 'official' Facebook and Twitter page; many also have Instagram. If you decide, as a middle leader, that this is appropriate for your department or year group then there are many benefits to this (providing that the senior leadership team have agreed). However, it is imperative to ensure that you have a policy in place if members of your department/year team are to be tweeting on behalf of the establishment that you all work for. This policy should provide useful guidelines, and a very clear outline of what is acceptable. There are risks at play when posting on behalf of a school, and any blurred lines could result in issues for your team members and thus for you and the school.

Top tips for social media

- Follow trusted accounts to begin with (@TES, @womened, @sltchat, @mltchat @teachmeeticons, for example).

- Don't feel that, because you're not a voice who is always on loud, you can't contribute. Your views and ideas matter as much as those of people with twenty thousand followers.

- Always speak to SLT prior to setting up a departmental/year group social media account and then create a very clear policy for usage.

- Avoid drawing comparisons between the accounts of colleagues on social media, and your real-life self.

- Behave online as you would in a meeting with colleagues.

- Stop and think prior to posting, because whatever you post on the internet will remain there forever.

- Follow the regular chats that are relevant to your area of leadership, often through hashtags (#Engchat, #SLTchat, #MLTchat, etc).

- Take the free resources, take **all** of the resources. But make them work for your context and ensure that you credit the creator.

- Work with SLT to ensure the social media policy is fair and fit for purpose – ideally before someone gets into trouble!

- Talk to your team about social media at the start of the school year and remind them of the school policy and potential pitfalls as well as positives.

12 | **Flexible working**

For a long time now, it seems like only a lucky few have been able to work flexibly in schools. Even then, part-time colleagues have sometimes been referred to as lazy, work-shy, and even having it easy at the expense of their harder-working colleagues. The phrase 'part-timer' is used with derision, the implication being that these colleagues are not quite pulling their weight. Thankfully, this attitude has begun to change, but it is slow progress. In 2019, 4.1 million people in the UK worked flexibly.[1] And that sounds like a lot, right? But actually compared to some nations we're not doing so well: Sweden has 71% of their workplaces offering flexible working; in the UK it's only 57%.[2] In teaching, these figures are even lower, with only 22% of UK teachers working flexibly. Around 8.6% of male teachers work part-time, compared to 13% of men in the workforce nationally, and the difference is even greater for women: 26.4% of female teachers work part-time, compared to 42% of women in the workforce nationally.[3]

Given that we have a recruitment and retention problem in teaching, surely it's a no-brainer to give the workforce what 87% of them want: flexible working. But actually, only 11% of jobs are advertised as being flexible.[4] All too often, school leaders only see the obstacles and downsides to flexible working, rather than the opportunities it brings. And as a middle leader, your influence is crucial in determining the climate of acceptance or blockage around these issues.

Case Study: Anonymous

Our school has generally been pretty accommodating of requests; We do have around 60% part-time staff in a large 1300 secondary just south of Mansfield.

We have four houses. One house has co-heads who do roughly three days each (although I think officially it's a three/two-day split but each finds it easier to spread their work over more days, as it's not more work). They have an excellent partnership, and feel that it helps them as, if one doesn't get on especially with a child/their parent, they have an alternative. They also have different personalities (one is a PE teacher, and one is an RE teacher) and although both are very kind and compassionate, they have different life experience and time in teaching (20 years and ten years). The co-headship was initially borne out of maternity leave years ago,

DOI: 10.4324/9781003160557-13

but when the job share moved on to become SENCO, this new dream team appeared, and I wish more jobs would be advertised as flexible/co-HOH.

The school gains too as they have two people for rotas, on-call duties, parents' evening points of reference, etc. It also gives the newer of the two the chance to develop the role whilst still working part-time while her children are young (5 and 3). Both teachers are part-time.

This year, I have spotted a way on the timetable where I can be more flexible, and the school has accepted it. So in Week 1, I will work four days: Monday, Tuesday, Thursday, Friday. But in Week 2, I still do my four days, but I will work Monday, Tuesday until lunch, then Wednesday afternoon, and all day on Thursday and Friday. This prevents a split on my Year 11s, but I think it will help me feel like I have more time outside of school (and my HOD says he won't let me stay on a Tuesday). It also means I can do the things I want to do: visit friends, read in my children's school (should it be allowed), read more – assuming that's ok again. But for me, working 0.8 of a timetable across five days, as my children are at school, prevents me just spending one whole day working at home unpaid – or so I hope! We will have to see if it goes to plan!

If you've ever enquired about working flexibly, chances are you've heard the following concerns from your leaders:

- ▉ You'd have to drop your TLR. What would that mean for your career?

- ▉ We can't timetable for that.

- ▉ We don't want split classes in this school, it's not good for the students.

- ▉ It's not the way we do things here; we want people who prioritise their job.

- ▉ How could you do parents' evenings if you don't work a Thursday?

- ▉ Who would have your tutor group?

- ▉ The kids would be confused.

- ▉ We can't afford to advertise for another teacher.

Essentially, a wave of negativity. And one which affects predominantly women and those with caring responsibilities (remember that the leadership demographic of our secondary schools is that 62% of Headteachers are men,[5] while 75% of the teaching workforce are women).[6]

But there is much to be said for flexible-working, and particularly now we have experienced Covid restrictions, they are becoming more evident to more people. Because of lockdown, we have become familiar with: Zoom meetings (with pets, children and sometimes confused parents or spouses wandering in or out of shot – a constant reminder that we all have lives and people to care for), remote teaching, and people having to be flexible and put family first – (no I can't meet at 9 am – my kids have the laptop for Joe Wicks!).

After lockdowns, we have seen the benefits of not always commuting in to the office, of embracing different technology to support our work, and in fact 61% of people wanted more working from home after lockdown.[7]

Case Study: Anonymous

I currently work flexibly in a secondary school teaching geography. My contract is 0.4 and I work that over two full days during which my partner works from home so does the school run enabling me to work long days. The days are pretty intense and there is a lot to achieve in that time but it works for me as I am able to manage the school run the rest of the week and take my children to clubs after school. I share a couple of classes with one colleague who is also part-time but mostly manage to have my own groups. Sharing classes is fairly smooth as we work off shared resources and I communicate clearly with my colleague over email. The school has worked out pro rata INSET so it is clear which days we need to attend. If they need us on a non-working day it is paid, offered remotely, or videoed. Department meetings alternate days so both part-time staff attend some. We also have a weekly department bulletin which ensures everyone has something to refer to if they need to check deadlines/ information. By offering this flexibility, the school has retained two experienced members of staff who would otherwise have left the profession.

Benefits of flexible working

Often flexible-working requests become bogged down in the difficulties and practicalities of school timetabling, so it's worth considering the benefits of flexible working to schools and organisations:

- Family-friendly/people-centred cultures help to retain and recruit talented people, and enhance discretionary effort. Higher levels of engagement, experienced by working flexibly, can reduce staff turnover by 87%.[8] Teachers near retirement might be retained for longer if allowed to work more flexibly.

- Flexible-working can help to reduce the gender pay gap by ensuring women keep their TLRs/leadership pay and continue to progress in their careers whilst working flexibly

- Government figures have shown that in 2017-18, 57% of all sick days were due to work-related stress, anxiety or depression[9]; so flexible working should result in reduced absences.

- Job shares can support the development of two or more people rather than one, plus more expertise and differing perceptions, which are factors in creating operational excellence.

▨ Students might experience two teachers' experience and knowledge in one subject, bringing twice the expertise and enthusiasm for their subject.

▨ Balancing the books: using curriculum-based-budgeting can mean there isn't always a need for full-time members of staff, and so flexible-working can help to trim extra staffing hours and help lower wage bills.

▨ Reputation: a school's image is created by word-of-mouth, and a reputation for supporting work-life balance can enhance its value as an employer, a big advantage when all schools are recruiting from the same small workforce pool.

▨ Increased productivity: research has repeatedly shown that productivity increases by 30% when employees work flexibly.

Case Study: Nicola Arkinstall Deputy Headteacher

I am a part-time Deputy Headteacher in a primary school in the Midlands. With the birth of my second daughter in 2013, it meant that I had two children under five years old. I had gone back to work full time after my maternity leave for my first daughter but felt that when returning the second time I wanted to explore the possibility of being able to work part-time in order to make it manageable and find some balance. My Headteacher was very supportive and agreed that I could return to work, three days a week. In order to make this work for the school and me, two Assistant Headteachers were appointed to take on some of my roles and responsibilities. This has had a real benefit for me and my school.

Initially, it allowed me to continue taking my daughter to baby activities and still feel like I was able to fulfil my role as a mum and a Deputy Head. Now, it means that, for two days a week, I can take my daughters and pick them up from school. This enables me to take them to after-school activities and have friends over to play. It also means that if there is a problem, like illness or school closures, we only have three days to sort out childcare for. It has also benefited my school because it enabled us to provide an opportunity for greater succession planning by appointing Assistant Headteachers. We have a much stronger senior leadership team which utilises the leadership talents of my colleagues.

Working part-time has also enabled me to have a number of opportunities I would not have been able to achieve if I was full-time. I am currently studying a Senior Leadership Masters with the National College of Education which I am finding really inspirational. I am also able to be a host on Teacher Hug Radio, where I present a show called 'Spotlight', which shines a light on schools and individuals who are doing amazing things in education. Next academic year, I will also be a Visiting Fellow to deliver the NPQs and ECF for local Teaching School Hubs. I am also able to find time to go to the gym and get all the household chores and appointments carried out. Having the time to study and take up interests supports me to perform at a higher level within my role. I am able to use what I have learned to develop initiatives within my school e.g. a school podcast.

It is vitally important to embrace flexible working in education to support the well-being of educators in order to enable them to thrive. If we enable our team to have *more of a work-life balance then when they are at work they will be able to give their best. It also ensures that quality people are retained and not lost from education. A more flexible approach improves retention, which is illustrated in schools who do embrace flexible working and the corporate world where this is commonplace. An empowering leader puts their staff first because they know that if they have a happy, healthy team this will ensure the best possible outcomes for their pupils.*

Overcoming obstacles

So what can leaders do, practically in schools, to overcome the obstacles which have for too long stood in the way of the embracing of flexible working?

- Timetabling: where there's a will, there's a way. And there are even free CPD courses to support people in timetabling for part-time workers.

- TLRs: why do people have to drop them? Make them pro-rata if necessary, and use it as a professional development opportunity for someone else to step up and lead whilst not having the full responsibility. Or, if the whole responsibility is still there, show that person that you value their time and expertise and pay them the full amount, as well as giving them the time to fulfil their role effectively.

- Culture: lead by example, use your words and your influence to celebrate flexible working. Have flexible working middle and senior leaders, men and women. Promote people who work flexibly. Refer to people's lives and families when you talk to them. Change the perception of PT by publicly acknowledging the organisation of those people and the flexibility and experience they bring to your school. Remember that your positive attitude influences others.

- Allow working from home. Why not? If the TT allows it, why not allow people to go home for their PPA? And if they choose to use that time to nip to the shops or take their kids to the park, then great! Embrace it and let them work flexibly - those reports can be written in an evening instead, if that's what works better for them. And they will respect your respect for their professionalism and autonomy.

In their report on flexible working in secondary schools, the NFER recommends the following:

- *The DfE should encourage the providers of leadership training (such as the National Professional Qualification for Headship and related qualifications) to develop content on adopting a proactive approach to part-time and flexible working. School leaders' attitudes and actions are critical to increasing opportunities for more flexible working*

If adopted, this is likely to have a positive impact on recruitment and retention, particularly in secondary schools where opportunities for flexible working are fewer than in primary.

▪ *The DfE should continue to prioritise reducing teacher workload and encouraging more flexible working in schools, including working with teacher organisations and middle-tier organisations, such as local authorities and MATs. This could include gathering and sharing of good practice and publicising the benefits for schools.*

Reductions to working hours should mean a corresponding reduction in workload, which is again another reason why teachers leave the profession.

▪ *School leaders should adopt a positive attitude towards encouraging part-time working, with flexibility on both sides. We recommend that school leaders adopt a proactive and systematic approach to encouraging flexibility for teachers whilst prioritising the needs of pupils. This includes seeking applications from all staff for part-time and flexible working.*

Recently more senior leaders have had access to CPD on timetable creation to allow for flexible working, and with generally improving IT systems in schools flexibility is more feasible on a logistical level than it has been previously.

▪ *Governors and school leaders should enable middle and senior leaders to adopt part-time working. Restricting leadership to those willing and able to work full-time limits the pool of leadership talent and means that teachers have to choose between leadership and part-time/flexible working.*

Flexible working for school leaders encourages a more diverse and therefore effective model of leadership, and is likely to encourage more women to apply for or stay in leadership positions in schools.

▪ *School leaders and policymakers should encourage more opportunities for flexible working among secondary teachers, beyond part-time working. This research found few examples of flexible working, as opposed to part-time working among teachers.[10]*

Barriers to flexible working such as needing to be on school premises during PPA or the inflexibility of timetables can be overcome, and the more schools and leaders that share examples of successful practice in this area the more likely it is to be seen as a valid and attainable working pattern.

Role of the middle leader in flexible working

Middle-leadership is crucial in ensuring the success of flexible working. You have the power to schedule meetings flexibly to ensure all can attend, or to use technology to include those working from home. You can liaise with SLT to support directed time calendars that suit staff working flexibly. As a part-time middle leader, you are an important visible signal that careers still flourish and that leadership works just as well when working flexibly. You can use email to ensure all communication and decisions are shared, including everyone, and send out bulletins so people can catch up at a time that suits them. Your role as an advocate and role model should not be underestimated – if you support flexible-working it is much more likely your SLT will be accommodating if they are undecided, and this will help to ensure the appreciation and loyalty of your team, as you advocate for their needs, as well as it bringing business benefits.

Case Study: J. Reiss Head of Key Stages Four and Five

Before I became pregnant with my first child, I had it all mapped out: 9 months' maternity leave, return to work full-time, kid would go to nursery four days a week and my mum's for one day. After all, we get stellar holidays and finish at three (lol), so I was practically working part-time anyway, right?

The issues at work started when I was pregnant; Shortly after telling work and my friends that I was expecting, I was called to the Deputy Head's office; the Head had heard that I had told people in a department meeting that I was pregnant before I had informed him. This apparently was A BAD THING, and I was rude and unprofessional for having done so. I tried to defend myself, saying that I had in fact informed the school first (true), and that I hadn't announced anything in a department meeting (also true), but it felt as though the tone had been set there and then.

As it turned out, there was a bit of a pregnancy boom that year; I think there were eleven of us, which was obviously going to be a bit of a staffing headache, even in a big school. But there didn't seem to be any protocols in place: there were no risk assessments done, and when one was eventually done I was asked to back-date the signature by three months so it looked like it had been done earlier. I was too scared to say no.

My HoD handed his notice in and took me aside, saying that if I hadn't been pregnant the school would have asked me to be the next HoD, but that pregnancy wasn't encouraged (in fact, I'm not sure being a woman at all was encouraged – there were so many rules and regulations on what we could and couldn't wear and say – down to dangly earrings being banned and at one point the wearing of pink was almost outlawed!), and to watch out – they wouldn't support me or let me go part-time. I laughed it off – I was returning full-time anyway.

Fast-forward a few months and I had my baby. Most thoughts of work were firmly relegated to the background as I tried to get through the most miserable, lonely and depressing period of my life; the baby was sick all the time. She cried ALL THE TIME. And I was alone most of the time. Being the first of my group of friends to have a child, even though I was 30, there was nobody else on maternity leave to share the time with. My family and husband all worked full-time. I went alone to baby groups (thank god for free Surestart activities in those days) and nobody spoke to me. I counted the hours until my husband came home. I couldn't do anything because we had no money, and I had no car as we sold mine to cut down on costs, so getting anywhere that wasn't on a bus route was impossible.

Despite, or maybe because of my misery, I was consumed by mummy guilt. This most special of precious times was flying by in an agony of endless hours, and it was almost time for me to start back at work again. And had I appreciated this time? Not one jot. And because the baby had been so ill, when she was almost nine months, she still hadn't done anything: no sitting up, no crawling, certainly no first steps – I was going back to work just as she was about to get interesting (or so I hoped).

After chatting it through with my husband, and looking at the extortionate cost of childcare, we worked out that if I went back to work three days a week, she could go to nursery two days and my mum's one day and we'd actually be no worse off than if I returned full-time and put her in nursery for four days. So I duly followed the flexible working guidance on the government website and applied to work part-time from the following September (not the current academic year as I didn't want to mess with their current timetabling). I had heard that sometimes these requests got rejected the first time (of course) but that usually won on appeal. But then I started to hear rumours: every person who had asked for flexible working this year had been turned down. I couldn't work out why – I mean timetabling would be a bit of a headache, but if it meant people could have a better work-life balance and the school got to keep happy and effective teachers, then why not?

I approached a couple of people from the school who already worked part-time: how did you manage it?

My baby is disabled so they allowed it.
I had two miscarriages so they allowed it.
My husband is on SLT so they allowed it.

When my request, like all the others, was rejected, I was upset but unsurprised. Also, I was furious. How dare they make a blanket decision to not allow any of us to work flexibly? How dare they dictate how I could prioritise my family? All the other women either accepted going back to work full-time, or resigned. I couldn't capitulate.

I contacted the union determined to fight it. Armed with stats and figures I went terrified to the appeal meeting with my rep, who confidently asserted that not one appeal in the county had ever been turned down. The meeting was fine, although they had brought a solicitor along which felt slightly intimidating. I was prepared to be totally flexible: I would work anywhere between two and four days a week. I would do any hours or split days. I would teach Monday mornings and Friday afternoons. I would have no GCSE classes. I would have all split classes. I would (naturally) drop my TLR. I would teach outside of my subject. Whatever they wanted, I would do.

Obviously, computer said no. I was invited in to see the Head for a chat. He knew I wasn't happy. As a 'goodwill gesture', if I decided to resign he would waive me paying back any of my maternity pay for not coming back at all.

I was depressed, terrified and anxious, but I decided to fight. How many other parents were going to be treated like this? On my return to work the week before May half term, I was given a full timetable, created by reducing everyone else's classes so

I was on 22 hours of teaching and everyone else was on 17 hours or fewer. One of my new classes had parents' evening on the second day and I was told I had to attend as their teacher. I hadn't even taught them. The final straw for me came when the timetable for September was 'accidentally' left on the printer by the second in department; I wasn't on it. I no longer taught at the school from September.

I returned to work, full-time, and at the same time wrote to the school letting them know I would be pursuing a case for sex discrimination and constructive dismissal. The union said I had a good case. After my letter had been received, I was phoned by the deputy head from the school down the road, who had just been taken over by the same Trust; would I like to come and be in charge of their KS4 and 5, part-time? Whatever hours I wanted? He had been contacted by my school and told I was a good teacher, and they needed good people.

I took the job. It suited us all – I got out of a toxic workplace, they got rid of a disruptive voice (don't get me started on all my reprimands for wearing pewter-coloured shoes or tights with patterns on), and I got to work flexibly AND keep my TLR.

In one sense I had 'won'; I got to work part-time, and for compassionate and ethical leaders who respected my choices. But the results of both the traumatic maternity leave plus the school's response on top were devastating to me personally; I felt suspicious of the motives of all leaders, I had no professional confidence, I couldn't make decisions, I lay awake at night sweating and wondering what people thought of me, I agonised over every conversation, replaying the minutiae of every day. I doubted my abilities in the classroom and as a leader. And of course I was a shit mum.

Eventually, through working with kind and trusting leaders, through lots of antidepressants and CBT, I got my mojo back. But it took years. And who knows where my career would have been if I hadn't got pregnant and incurred the wrath of the school? And more importantly maybe I wouldn't have been so miserable for so long.

For me the case study above has a clear moral message: leaders in school can make you or break you. We want to be leaders who make people. What do you want to be?

Top tips on creating a culture for flexible working as a middle leader

- Lead by example: model flexible working e.g. notes on your email acknowledging different working patterns, or working flexibly yourself to show it can be done.

- Support the logistics: arrange meetings so they don't exclude, and employ supportive practices such as sending out weekly bulletins. Be open to split classes and sharing projects in your team to support flexible workers.

- Talk it up: be positive and open when talking to staff and senior leaders. Yes there will be difficulties, but they are never insurmountable, and your voice carries weight.

◼ Don't assume: just because someone has had a child that doesn't mean they will want to alter their working pattern. Someone without caring responsibilities might want to work flexibly just as much or more as those with caring responsibilities.

Notes

1 Office for National Statistics (ONS). (March 2020). Coronavirus and homeworking in the UK labour market. (2019). https://www.ons.gov.uk/employmentandlabourmarket/peopleinwork/employmentandemployeetypes/articles/coronavirusandhomeworkingintheuklabourmarket/2019

2 CIPD (June 2019). Flexible Working in the UK, https://www.cipd.co.uk/Images/flexible-working_tcm18–58746.pdf

3 Department for Education. (December 2020). Flexible Working in Schools, https://www.gov.uk/government/publications/flexible-working-in-schools/flexible-working-in-schools--2

4 Timewise Flexible Jobs Index. (2018). https://timewise.co.uk/wp-content/uploads/2018/07/Timewise_ Flexible_Jobs_-Index_2018.pdf quality jobs defined a £20k +FTE

5 Oxford Open Learning (OOL). (April 2018). Gender Diversity in Schools, https://www.ool.co.uk/blog/gender-diversity-in-schools/

6 Gov.UK. (February 2021). School Teacher Workforce, https://www.ethnicity-facts-figures.service.gov.uk/workforce-and-business/workforce-diversity/school-teacher-workforce/latest

7 Deloitte. (n.d.). Working During Lockdown, https://www2.deloitte.com/uk/en/pages/consulting/articles/working-during-lockdown-impact-of-covid-19-on-productivity-and-wellbeing.html

8 Institute for Employment Studies & The Work Foundation. (2018). People and the bottom line: https://www. employment-studies.co.uk/system/files/resources/files/448.pdf

9 Health and Safety Executive (HSE). (November 2020). Work-related stress, anxiety or depression statistics in Great Britain, 2020 https://www.hse.gov.uk/statistics/causdis/stress.pdf

10 National Foundation for Educational Research (NFER). (2019). Part-time Teaching and Flexible Working in Secondary Schools.

Bibliography

CIPD. (June 2019). Flexible Working in the UK, https://www.cipd.co.uk/Images/flexible-working_tcm18–58746.pdf

Deloitte. (n.d.). Working During Lockdown, https://www2.deloitte.com/uk/en/pages/consulting/articles/working-during-lockdown-impact-of-covid-19-on-productivity-and-wellbeing.html

Department for Education. (December 2020). Flexible Working in Schools, https://www.gov.uk/government/publications/flexible-working-in-schools/flexible-working-in-schools--2

Gov.UK. (February 2021). School Teacher Workforce, https://www.ethnicity-facts-figures.service.gov.uk/workforce-and-business/workforce-diversity/school-teacher-workforce/latest

Health and Safety Executive. (2018). Work-related stress, anxiety or depression Institute for Employment Studies & The Work Foundation, People and the bottom line: https://www.employment-studies.co.uk/system/files/resources/files/448.pdf.

National Foundation for Educational Research (NFER). (2019). Part-time Teaching and Flexible Working in Secondary Schools.

Office for National Statistics (ONS). (March 2020). Coronavirus and Homeworking in the UK Labour Market: 2019, https://www.ons.gov.uk/employmentandlabourmarket/peopleinwork/employmentandemployeetypes/articles/coronavirusandhomeworkingintheuklabourmarket/2019

Oxford Open Learning (OOL). (April 2018). Gender Diversity in Schools, https://www.ool.co.uk/blog/gender-diversity-in-schools/

Statistics in Great Britain. (2020). https://www.hse.gov.uk/statistics/causdis/stress.pdf, HSE, November 2020.

Timewise Flexible Jobs Index (2018): https://timewise.co.uk/wp-content/uploads/2018/07/Timewise_Flexible_Jobs_-Index_2018.pdf quality jobs defined a £20k +FTE

13   Positive disruption

What does it mean to be positively disruptive as a middle leader? To us, it means to use your position to support the senior leaders in your school to make the right decisions, by offering your voice on behalf of your team, and as somebody also still on the front line in the classroom. It is the responsibility of every middle leader to both support and challenge decisions made by SLT, and this is what we mean by positive disruption.

In our experience, middle leaders are sometimes assumed to be 'yes wo/men' to the SLT. However, if this is the case then who, apart from governors (who are often removed from the day-to-day running of a school) will give feedback to and ask questions of SLT on a daily basis? And, even if the school is part of a multi-academy trust, the CEO/Director will not be able to be at the school as consistently as those working within it, and so somebody has to be able to open and maintain that dialogue about the day-to-day running of the school, and that responsibility likely falls to the middle leaders.

As main scale teachers, we sometimes wondered what the role of middle leaders really was. What were they really privy to? How much voice did they actually have? And what power did they have to challenge senior decisions? The fact that we needed to ask these questions made us aspire to be a middle leader because we wanted to effect change. We didn't want to continue to see what we sometimes witnessed: a disconnect between the wants of SLT and the needs of those in the classrooms – not that there is one in all schools, but there certainly is in some. A middle leader joins together the classroom teachers who are probably teaching at capacity, and those in SLT who might be drowning under competing pressures such as analysing data to death, or trying to identify a cure for failing exam results/ poor behaviour/staff turnover….

Middle leaders teach; we lead CPD; we write curriculum; we meet with SLT. We, forgive me for sounding crude, have our fingers in every pie. Therefore, as we wrote about in the chapter on Ethical Leadership, it is important that as middle leaders we draw on our expertise; are aware that we do not always just say yes to every request; and that we are empowered to be 'disruptive voices' who will challenge, question, and try to improve decisions and plans that we truly do not agree with, or believe in, or see as flawed.

DOI: 10.4324/9781003160557-14

Case Study: K. Donald, Head of Languages

A headteacher at a school that I once worked at insisted on using 'feedback sessions' for students at lunchtime. To begin immediately. The new specification had just launched, and everybody was panicking. Lunchtime at this school was short, so the proposal meant that students were given ten minutes to collect and eat their lunch, before they were expected to be back in a classroom. There was no specific focus, just to use the time to feedback what they needed to know as a summary of feedback from that week of teaching and learning.

When the concept was proposed in a leadership meeting, it seemed that the long-standing middle leaders were all nodding along, whilst another curriculum leader and I locked eyes and shared a look of disbelief. Here, it would have been easy for us both to agree and then take it to the staff room and complain. But what impact would that have had? It was time to manage up, and provide some positive disruption:

"Sorry," I remarked, "But what is the point?"

Everybody in the room looked shocked. It was clear that this sort of challenge wasn't the norm in this particular context.

"Forgive me. Let me explain my question," I elaborated. "If it is for all students, and we have no particular focus, how do we use this time effectively? Why are we asking every student in every class to attend these sessions weekly?"

"But, if we are showing the students that we will give up our time at lunch to support them, then we are showing our willing and therefore they will engage better," explained a member of SLT.

"With all due respect, I have to disagree. I can't see how this is going to have any positive impact; if anything, it will disengage the students. There's also the matter of when exactly my team are going to eat."

The 'feedback sessions' went ahead as planned the following week, but it was clear that the students and staff were disgruntled and that the way the sessions were running was having very little positive impact, if any at all. I continued to challenge the concept with my line manager where I suggested potential solutions, and my line manager fed back the concerns to the head.

"So I've spoken to [head] about your issues with the new feedback sessions, and we've decided to use an analysis of formative assessment over time inform them in more detail. Also, groups will be no more than eight students in one session post-Christmas. We thought long and hard about the issues that you raised, and the solutions you offered and we do think that would be the best way to move forward with compulsory sessions at lunchtime."

"Okay, but there's still the issue about engagement and when staff and students will eat, isn't there? What is the proposal for change on this aspect?"

"Well, it's a case of having to just put up with a couple of lunch sessions a week, I'm afraid."

In my line management meetings, I could have just complained and said that the sessions weren't working, that my team were unhappy that they were being directed to give up their lunchtimes, and that the students hated it. However, that would have done little good. Instead, I presented solutions to the problem that these sessions seemed to be bringing about; I provided a question-level analysis of the cohort's most recent independent work.

The lunchtime feedback sessions became much more focussed, we allowed students and staff to eat lunch in the classrooms which brought about a much more relaxed feel, and the impact of these sessions was significantly more positive than they had been with the initial set-up.

To be an effective middle leader is not, simply, to be a middle wo/man. We are so much more than that. We don't carry messages like the wartime pigeons, from one side of the school building where SLT live, to the other where the teachers reside. We critique, dissect, question and analyse at senior level; we should return it to the sender, and keep doing so until it is the right message to deliver, or at least the best compromise that can be made.

Generally, middle leaders get paid a significant TLR, or find ourselves on the Leadership Scale. We are not paid this salary to unquestioningly do as we are told by those senior to us. Of course, we have to advocate and present as a united front with our SLT the minute that we walk out of those conference room doors, but that's not to say that we didn't sit for an hour asking them about their decision, breaking it down into multiple components and looking at it from an array of perspectives: how does this impact the staff body? Our ECTs and trainees, how will they handle this directive? What impact will this have on the students? How are parents going to receive this? What about our part-time team members; can we be more flexible? Where are we reducing workload, if we are adding something else? Will this work? How? Which members of staff could we bring on board with this initiative to empower them? Who, amongst our staff body, could lead on aspects of this? How will this impact behaviour and engagement in lessons? Hopefully, SLT has thought carefully through all of this, but our perspective may well highlight areas that had been missed, and your SLT may well be thanking you for the catch at the end of this discussion.

It is our job to challenge, professionally disagree with, to highlight flaws in a plan, and to offer solutions to any problems that we identify. If we don't, we are not doing middle leadership right. We have to do middle leadership right, for the whole school to get it right.

For any team to be effective, including schools and the leadership groups within them, disruptive voices in the 'engine room' are crucial; throwing new and innovative fuel on the fire, making others see their own plans in another light. The headteacher may well be at station control, and the SLT have their hands on the buttons, but it is middle leaders that are the driving force behind any school vehicle and that is why it is so important to empower them, and to value their insights about everything that they are consulted about: from behaviour to pedagogy, from staff wellbeing to seating plans. Middle leaders can be schools' strongest tool.

Case Study: T. Holmes, Secondary Head of Year

I have lost count of the times I have been advised to be more measured in my opinion, to be quieter in meetings, to be softer, gentler, less formidable even. Reflecting on the numerous times I have received advice of this kind, always by more senior female colleagues, I genuinely believe the guidance came from places of kindness and a belief that this feedback was a gift to aid my development, like sharing a secret recipe for success. Sadly, it seemed being a more successful colleague meant I needed to play a role which allowed me to be accepted (liked even), and therefore I must be less assertive, and less formidable.

Opposing advice paints a more illuminating picture of how I "should" behave professionally. "Be more emotional, more human, show vulnerability." It has even been suggested that I should be "less calm in a crisis." The common theme of the feedback I have received is to modify my behaviour to fall within the stereotypical bounds of a young, aspiring female leader: essentially, my behaviour makes others feel uncomfortable. An openly aspirational female is not celebrated like a male, but viewed with suspicion. I have been accused of not being student-focused, that I should stand back from successful initiatives I have led, or that many hours of hard work on a charitable community project is because I want a promotion or to claim the 'glory.' This is criticism I don't often hear levelled at my male colleagues. In my limited experience, females who work hard, who hold (and dare to share) strong opinions, and who are openly ambitious are held to different moral standards than their male counterparts.

The female colleagues who have offered me advice about how to be more successful in education leadership are inspirational leaders, women I look up to, women whom I aspire to emulate. I have deliberately stayed silent during meetings in the guise of being softer, quieter and more amiable, but I didn't feel more accepted; I felt fake. I felt as though I were playing a part and not being true to myself — fraudulent almost. I was behaving in a manner that made others feel at ease, but I felt deeply uncomfortable. Actually, I felt incompetent.

The irony is that my assertive nature, my confidence, my courage and my ambition is my strength. Yes, it makes others uncomfortable, but not because I am unkind or mean. I hope never to be that colleague. They feel uncomfortable because I ask the difficult questions others shy away from. I recognise that I have much to learn about leading in education, and I work hard on improving myself as a human, but I am not willing to constrain my natural strengths in order to fit others' ideas of how I should be. I want to be the best version of myself for the students, staff and community I serve.

I know that historically the only way women could step up into leadership was to behave in the expected gendered stereotypical fashion or to assimilate with stereotypical male characteristics. Things do not have to be like this anymore...

In the words of John Tomsett, 'this much I know' about challenging the pervasive outdated means of reaching the upper echelons of educational leadership. It is for the benefit of all the women who follow us: we must break and reshape the mould for those who will succeed us.

So what's the alternative? As a current, and future, female leader in education I will offer younger, less experienced leaders the advice I wish I'd received, whether they're male or female. The two pieces of advice I will give to the next generation of leaders will be these: 1. Serve your students, staff and community with your own personal strengths; 2. Do not bend or alter who you are because your strengths remind others of their own latent insecurities. Your school needs you to be you at your most impressive, not you at your most subservient.

Team expertise

What does this mean if you're a senior leader reading this? Talk to your middle leaders and respect their specific areas of expertise, and take them into account when making decisions and strategising. For example, maybe you're the Head of Teaching and Learning, but have you asked how direct instruction works in Maths, and then made a direct comparison with that in English and History? Perhaps you're the Head of Whole School Literacy, but have you asked the Head of Science how they incorporate academic language in order to work towards closing the disadvantage gap; the Head of Maths how he feels about Drop Everything and Read and its impact on his subject, which they feel is wholly divided from the literacy programme? You might be in charge of pastoral care and student welfare, but have you asked the Head of Art how his/her subject could be drawn upon for those struggling to verbalise their emotions, or the Head of English how academically challenging texts support students' behaviour through the means of achievement as motivation?

These middle leaders are your eyes and ears on the ground. Empower them by drawing on their expertise; show them that you value them by drawing on their opinions, and prove that you trust them by handing them autonomy to work with you.

Just as middle leaders are not simply middle wo/men, members of the SLT are not one-man-bands. To be effective, we must work together as a solid body of leadership who all draw on the expertise of one another. We will disagree, and a decision may well be made or a plan may well go ahead that one of us doesn't wholly agree with, but, as long as everybody's voice has been heard and considered – important for ethical leadership – when we go in front of that staff body, we are a united front. We advocate for whatever the final decision was, with professionalism and with pride.

Professionally disruptive

So, how do we remain positively disruptive without – well – pissing people off, and maintaining professional integrity? If there is a problem to identify, offer a solution. Don't simply complain, or disagree. Back it up with solid research. As Emma Turner once said at WomenEd Unconference 2018 – 'be more marigold' and spread positivity.

Nobody likes somebody in meetings who argues for the sake of argument, and nobody doing middle leadership right will be that person. Middle leaders and SLT are a team, and there is no place for hierarchy or egos in this. Effective middle leaders should not be afraid of appropriately challenging SLT, and an effective SLT should not feel threatened or insulted when their middle leaders do so.

So how do we eradicate this concept of toxic hierarchy within schools? We build trust, on both sides. We challenge where we deem necessary, but never personally. We disagree where we deem necessary but always explain. We offer solutions to problems. We say no where necessary but always provide rationale.

Have we been perceived as 'difficult' in situations where we have questioned SLT or, prior to our time as a middle leader, when questioning middle leaders? Yes! It's a huge part of who we are to advocate for what we truly believe in. Have we always gone about it in the most professional of ways? God no. But we've learnt from these mistakes, we've learnt that, sometimes, SLT are too busy to consider the multiple implications of a situation and have to look at the holistic viewpoint, and that by providing our school leaders with more detailed insights, we are supporting them. Whilst it may initially come across as 'difficult', it isn't if it is done in the right way – politely, professionally and usually privately. In the long term, positive disruption from middle leaders has a much more positive impact than simply saying yes.

Middle leaders don't challenge things that they disagree with simply to be difficult. And SLT will recognise this. It is our job to ensure that under achievement of whichever classes/subjects we are in charge of is tackled. If you don't think that an SLT initiative is the most effective way of doing so, then tell them. More likely than not, they'll appreciate it. Bring research and solutions to the table, though, don't just bitch and moan about it.

Compromise

It's important to note that, by challenging, you won't get everything that you want for your team and students. You'll most likely have to reach some sort of compromise, and that's perfectly okay. You might not be overly pleased with some of the final decisions, but you have to walk out of the meetings in which such decisions are made final, and make it your own. To your team, you and your SLT are one team; it would be disconcerting for them if that wasn't the case. You need to reassure your team that, whilst you 'have their back', you also align with the SLT of your school. A disjointed leadership is never fun or games for a team below them.

Often, it will take some reflection on an agenda item before you even realise the issues that you – and others – might have with it. If you see a problem, you must work towards a solution. There's no good just saying no and stomping your feet hoping that SLT will cave and give you what it is that you think is right. Ask questions, reflect and then bring solutions; this is where middle leaders can be helpful for time-stretched SLT, who will, as a result, be more likely to listen.

A good SLT will communicate with middle leaders whenever possible prior to making any decision that will impact them and their teams (which, in a school, is almost every decision), often via SLT and ML line management meetings. If that isn't the case in your school, then this is perhaps the first thing you should ask about and pose as a solution for making initiatives and communication run more smoothly.

Equally, just as SLT will consult their middle leadership, middle leaders must draw on their own teams – from ITT participants to veteran teachers – and value every single voice that they hear. Whilst the buck stops with you, you will never get your team on board with your vision if you simply make all the decisions by yourself. It is imperative to autonomise staff of all levels, in order for wellbeing to be strong and for people to feel empowered and valued as professionals – more on this in the chapters on ethical leadership and difficult conversations.

If you're reading this and you can recognise some of the qualities of somebody being seen as 'difficult', ask yourself the following question: Is it them being difficult, or is it a positively disruptive voice that you need to hear? Without the challenges that they proposed, would you have moved forward with an initiative or made a decision that was – unbeknownst to you – flawed? Has that voice that you previously categorised as 'difficult', actually, just shone a pretty bright light on a dark corner of your plan that you hadn't even considered?

Rather than roll your eyes, switch off, or get frustrated with the middle leader in your extended leadership meeting who seems to find a problem with everything, listen to them, and actually make note of what they are saying. It often takes a fresh pair of eyes and ears to see and hear what it is that won't work, even when something has been toiled over for weeks and weeks. It's not dissimilar to when a writer pays somebody to proof the work that they've been drafting for a year: that proofreader is far better able to spot the errors made by a writer who only reads what they intended to write. Flaws, errors and issues with what we believe to be some of our best work are so much easier to spot when looked at by eyes belonging to those who are not as personally and emotionally attached to the prototype as what we are.

Retaining staff

What happens if SLT doesn't buy into the positively disruptive voices? If school leaders can't change their perspective of the 'difficult' members of their teams, and simply don't listen? Well, frankly: they are likely to lose them.

When middle leaders, or any member of staff, are appointed, no matter the size of their TLR or their point on the L scale, if they are not listened to or valued then they will not stick around. No effective teacher goes into educational middle leadership simply for the money. They do it to have an impact to a wider scope than their classroom. If that doesn't happen, and if SLT are the ones to make all the decisions, then they will seek roles whereby they are given the opportunities to impact whole-school decisions. It truly is that simple.

Many schools and SLTs are already doing this, and brilliantly, but for those who aren't it's time to set egos aside, to forget about hierarchy (to an extent, of course) and accept that SLT need middle leaders to challenge decisions, to highlight issues that may arise, to advocate for the wider staff body (which sometimes, without meaning to, SLT are subconsciously distanced from), and to offer alternative paths towards an agreed, whole-school vision. By allowing, and encouraging the middle leadership team to do all of the above, we can be assured that directives and initiatives are being fed back to the wider staff body with confidence, solidarity and where middle leaders have the answers to all queries that staff may throw their way.

Now, it's important to know that we are not advocating for being that member of the team that argues with every single point. As Andy Hope once said in a 'Pathways to Leadership' course that we attended as an RQT, 'nobody needs a mood hoover'. Positively disruptive voices are not the mood hoovers. They have reason and rationale behind every single challenge that they raise, and they do so to support school leadership in being its most effective. They are the opposite of moaning for moaning's sake, and they will be the messengers of your vision, as long as your vision is theirs too.

Conclusions on positive disruption

So, a message to SLT (aspiring or current): get middle leader buy-in by listening to their voices and acting on their concerns. You cannot run a school by yourself, you need them. You cannot be in every single classroom, or have a daily conversation with every single classroom teacher. Your middle leaders can. Hone their expertise, value their insight and gain their trust.

Now, a message to middle leaders (aspiring or current): don't be afraid to raise issues with something asked of you, don't be afraid to say no: remember that you are not a middle wo/man. You are a middle leader, and that does not mean doing everything that is asked of you unquestioningly. You're the teacher equivalent of that child who offers an alternative route to work out a difficult equation than the teacher, and shares it with his friends. You're the teacher equivalent of that child who provides an alternative interpretation of a line of poetry, and raises her hand to challenge her teacher. You are a positively disruptive voice who endeavours to be so in order to ensure the school is led in the most effective manner possible.

And finally, a message to both: fight it out, professionally debate and go back and forth as much as possible behind closed doors. But the minute you walk out of those doors, you do so together: you are a team – a united front. You are the reason for your staff's confidence in the school and its leadership.

Top tips on positive disruption

- If there is a problem to identify, offer a solution. Don't simply complain, or disagree. Back it up with solid research.

- Listen carefully and take notes.

- Leave your ego at the door – other people will have better ideas than you or will improve yours, and that's as it should be – that's teamwork.

Common pitfalls, and debunking myths

Lyndsay: When I first became a middle leader, I had absolutely no idea what that really entailed. When I worked in a pastoral role, I knew that I would have to keep track of attendance, give assemblies (gah!), speak to parents and carers more, and give more tellings off. When I became an HoD, I knew that meant I had to make sure the GCSE results went up, and I got to pick which topics we taught. That was about it really. If you're reading this and wondering why anyone ever gave me a TLR then you might have a valid point! But really I wonder if any of us have a full picture of what leadership is like before we actually do it. No matter how long we might have worked in schools for, and how carefully we might have observed those around us, it's not until that responsibility really becomes ours, and we have to live in and do that job everyday, that the full reality of it really hits home.

Jade: Becoming a middle-leader as an RQT was a very daunting experience. I was barely formed as a teacher, let alone knowing anything about leadership! I'm not sure that I had misconceptions so much as just didn't know anything at all. I did think that it was going to be a lot easier than it was though. In some ways, I thought I would be more autonomous: I thought that I was going to be able to make decisions without having to worry too much about those above me, or in my team, because I assumed that we would all want the same thing. In other ways, I thought that there would be much more support: that I would be given more guidance on handling difficulties, data and development. I was wrong on both counts!

Kaley: Nobody ever told me what to expect as a middle leader. I had the interview, was successful and then that was it really: I just did it. I had to make assumptions about what the job entailed, and some of those assumptions turned out to be completely inaccurate. I look back at some of my preconceptions of my many roles within middle leadership and have a bit of a laugh at myself now.

DOI: 10.4324/9781003160557-15

As second in department, I assumed that I would be a general dog's body to the Head of Department, not that I would be expected to analyse KS3 data in depth and report back to them on my findings! As Head of Department, I assumed that I had to raise student progress and improve the curriculum, but I never once thought that I'd have to be creating evidence folders for the teacher assessed grades in place of official exams during a global pandemic. As Head of House, I assumed I'd be giving assemblies and rollockings. I didn't consider the time I'd be expected to spend on analysing behaviour data and writing reports for the SLT in charge of personal development.

Common pitfalls, and debunking myths

This final chapter of the book is about identifying and addressing some of the common illusions we have about middle leadership, and how to deal with what the reality is really like. Hopefully, it'll support you as aspiring/current middle leaders to understand the reality that comes with a middle leadership role, whilst also making you laugh at the naive moments from our own middle leadership positions.

Time

Preconception: My extra frees are going to make my life so much easier!
The reality: Everyone wants a piece of you and you are never left alone to get anything done. 'Can you just' becomes your most hated phrase.
Solution: Be organised with yourself and others. Make lists and set up systems. Prioritise carefully and don't waste your own time by flicking through social media on your PPA. Get your lessons prepped the week before; set aside daily time slots to read and respond to emails, and, if really desperate, find somewhere to hide so you can work undisturbed (but not too much, as you have to be visible and accessible to your team). Try saying: *I'm really glad you've asked me about this. Can we make time to talk about it properly tomorrow? I want to give you my full attention.*

Power

Preconception: I will now be able to solve all the problems in the school that have been bugging me and others.
The reality: Trying to do everything for everyone and being everything for everyone means you spread yourself thin and do nothing well. Paperwork is endless! Risk assessments, stock audits, return to work forms, exam analysis reports, support plans, attendance and behaviour analysis...
Solution: Say no to things. You might be new to your role and it's hard to say no when someone asks you for help, but sometimes you have to prioritise, and

sometimes people need to be empowered to do things themselves. Ask: *do you have a suggestion as to how we can solve this? Great! Can you speak to XX about it please?* Or, *I know this is a really important issue but right now we need to focus on XX. Let's come back to this after Christmas.*

Talking to the head

Preconception: I'm too lowly for them to bother with me
The reality: They really want to know what you're doing and how you're getting on because you're a valuable employee.
Solution: Make the most of your new position to communicate the key ideas and issues they need to know. Go into meetings with notes so you don't forget what you want to say, and solutions to issues.

   Or

Preconception: I'll be going on holiday with the Head now I've been promoted
The reality: They're really busy and you've not had a line-management meeting for months
Solution: Speak to their PA and see if you can set up weekly/fortnightly meetings. Copy them into your team emails so you're keeping them in the loop. If all else fails, loiter outside their toilet and pounce.

Accountability

Preconception: I don't get stressed so the pressure won't get to me
The reality: you wake up in a cold sweat worrying if you're going to meet next week's deadlines.
Solution: Be kind to yourself and accept that the first year in a new role will be daunting as it's unknown so you will worry more – it's normal. Speak to your line manager about workload and deadlines. Remember that a school is a team and no one person is responsible for anything alone. We work together and there are people to help if you need it. Be fair and reasonable – don't take your stress out on others.

People

Preconception: My only focus is going to be the students
The reality: You can't get anything done because of staffroom fall-outs, questions, absences, too much laughing in the office, supporting Jamie after he broke up with his boyfriend...
Solution: How much people management is involved in leadership is often underestimated, but try to remember that the people you work with are the talent of the school. Look after your team and they will look after the students. Bring

tissues, bake cakes and be kind. Accept good days and bad days, but hold others to account. Model the behaviour, kindness and professionalism you want to see.

Resistance

Preconception: Everyone will respect me and my new authority
The reality: respect has to be earned, and even then some won't give it
Solution: Don't set yourself up to fail by making unreasonable requests, not consulting people, and not communicating. Talk through the rationale for decisions and explain why things are important. Ask for your team's views. Speak 1-1 with people if you anticipate difficulties to head them off. If all else fails, don't be afraid to ask for support from your line manager.

Them and us

Preconception: nothing will change and I can still be BFFs with everyone
The reality: some people might see you as an authority figure, won't be your friend, and won't confide in you.
Solution: Accept this difference and respect people's rights to set boundaries on relationships. But, also work to reassure people. Act ethically, respect people, and trust them, and you will earn trust in return.

Case Study on losing a friendship: G Hutchinson, Assistant Head of Curriculum

On being promoted to a more senior role within the department, I expected that nothing would change amongst the friends within my collegiate circle. I'd been working with this team for six years, and we socialised outside of work almost every weekend.

However, what I was unprepared for was the fact that my own friends of five and six years would start to distance themself from me just because of my new, more senior title of 'Assistant Leader of Curriculum'. I started to take notice of the fact that I wasn't invited to social events as I would have done when I was 'just' a teacher, that the group chat had gone quiet of late, and that the conversations that used to take place in the department office seemed to have lulled.

I realised that none of this was my doing, but the doing of leaders before me who had set a precedent that professional hierarchy comes before personal friendships. I tried not to take it personally, but I would be lying if I pretended that it didn't upset me.

Instead of wallowing, I decided that I'd set a new precedent: just because I'm now responsible for aspects of the curriculum, doesn't mean that I can't be the friend that I had been for years to some members of my team; just because I often have to have difficult conversations with people professionally doesn't mean that I can't know them personally.

Of course, there is always going to be the issue of potentially blurred boundaries and it's important that you model the behaviour that you wish to see in your team. But just because you become 'the boss' doesn't mean that you can't also be 'the friend'. The two are not mutually exclusive, and as long as it is made clear that there are professional expectations between you and your team members (as there are with all colleagues) then you'll be able to trust and be trusted.

Did I remain friends with everybody that I was friends with previously? No. There were a few members of the department who, because I was their friend, expected me to gloss over some really quite serious issues: drinking heavily and coming to work still intoxicated was just one issue that I had to address with one of these said 'friends'. If people expect you to do things that put your professional integrity at risk, instead of being happy for your successful promotion to a new leadership role, they are not your friends. Whilst it may well be a hard pill to swallow to begin with, you should never be expected to put yourself at risk in order to protect others. They are professionals, as are you, and they should act as such.

Money, money, money....

Preconception: I'm going to have a budget and will buy all the pastel highlighters I have ever dreamed of!

The reality: Who knew budgets and finance were so complicated?

Solution: Sit down with someone from finance and ask them to show you how the finance system works. Make LOTS of notes. Keep a running track of your budget and don't blow it all at the start. Speak to your line manager about unexpected costs. Don't spend every penny at the end of the year just because it's there – remember that that money is there for the benefit of the students, and another department might really need that extra you have spare.

Case Study: F. Field Head of English

Recently appointed as Head of Department, I found myself with a pot of money to spend. As it always does when I'm paid, the money was seemingly burning a hole in my pocket. I was given free reign to spend money at will, so who was I to not log into the ESPO catalogue and buy *all of the things*?

Pastel highlighters? Check. Border roll in abundance? Check. Backing paper for *all of the displays?* I'll take twenty-three! Victorian school backdrop to use when delivering Victorian Literature? Check. Check. Check.

Were all of these resources necessary? Could I have spent more responsibly? Was the budget tight at the end of the year as a result? Yes, yes, and yes.

We have to remember, even when given a pot of money that isn't really ours to spend, that we are spending public funds and these must be spent wisely. Invest in quality CPD for your team, in quality enrichment for your students.

But never spend for the sake of spending. I am mortified to say that, in my whole time as Head of Department, those border rolls never did run out and that Victorian school backdrop never once came out of the cardboard tubing!

Running meetings

Preconception: Everyone will love coming to my meetings because I will bring biscuits.

The reality: I am in my fifth meeting of the week and it's only Tuesday.

Solution: Could this meeting have been an email? No, really. If it's procedural then send out a weekly bulletin. What could your meeting time really be best used for? Not sure – ask your team how they want to use the time. Do you have to use every minute or can the last half be given over to people to go and do something constructive or to action a priority? What does your team really need right now – if it's not this meeting, then re-schedule it. Trust them to use the time wisely.

Making a massive cock-up

Preconception: Obviously I'm not going to make that mistake, duh!

The reality: Shit. …

Solution: Be honest and tell someone more senior straight away. Whatever it is will only be made worse by lying or hiding it. Act ethically and do the right thing. And remember: everyone makes mistakes; it's how we handle them that counts.

Case Study: Anonymous

In my first year as Head of Department, one of my duties was to enter all the students for their GCSEs in my subject. This was quite a tricky process, as the electronic tracking system we used was always wrong, and because we were below PAN there seemed to be a constant influx of new students to the school, meaning registers were frequently changing. On top of this, we had an off-site Alternative Provision as part of the school, and some students at the AP had been there for years – I had never met them and they weren't on any of my trackers.

The procedure was that I submitted the lists of entries to the Exams Officer, who worked between two schools so didn't know our students particularly well, they sent it back to us to check, and I would send it to each teacher in the department to check and sign to ensure that all their students were there and had been put in for the correct tier of paper.

On the day of the exam, the Exams Officer came to see me to say that there weren't enough exam papers, and that there were students in the exam hall who weren't on the seating plan. She asked what had happened and I had no idea. I went to the hall to see these students (we were allowed in the room in those days) and there were some students there I had never seen before!

It turned out that there were students in the school who had been missed off from the class lists and not entered, and neither I nor the class teacher had noticed, and that none of the AP students had been entered either.

The Exams Officer called the exam board who said that they didn't take late exam entries and these students couldn't sit the exam. In desperation, we photocopied one of the papers and all the students sat the exam anyway in the hope that something could be done afterwards (they didn't know anything about the behind-the-scenes panic!). I went to see the Head and told her straight away what had happened. She called the exam board and basically begged for their papers to be marked, and the board eventually relented after charging us triple entry fees for each student.

I was asked to speak to the Head. I explained that the error was mine, that the lists had been submitted by me, and that it was my responsibility. I know that I could have complained about the systems (which were later changed so that this didn't happen again) or blamed the class teacher who had missed off her students, or pointed the finger at SLT who hadn't put processes in place for the AP students, but I felt it was the right thing to do to just accept that a mistake had been made and that the accountability for it stopped with me. It was never mentioned again by SLT, despite me fearing that I would be sacked for such incompetence!

Afterwards, the class teacher who had missed off some of their students came to thank me for not mentioning their name and 'getting them into trouble'; remembering that makes me feel like I did the right thing by taking responsibility and not looking to shift the blame elsewhere.

Data

Preconception: I'm going to be trained to become an Excel whiz and I will be using macros, if statements and pivot tables like an absolute boss within the first term.
The reality: What are all these numbers on the page and why are they written in a code beginning with =?
Solution: Draw on your school data manager; these people are wizards and it is literally their job to support you with the creation of spreadsheets and data analysis that makes sense to you.

Behaviour

Preconception: The students will be able to smell my leadership as I walk around the school and will automatically respect me and bow to my presence when I enter a room.
The reality: No, no they will not. Relationships with students and the respect that comes from these relationships is not automatic because you got a promotion.

You must earn their trust and respect and your presence will be the only thing to do so.

Solution: Be present. Go in and out of classrooms, supporting your team members and their classes. Have conversations with children in the corridor about what they are learning in your subject. Take an interest in them, and really care. Be consistent in your rules and expectations.

The voice of the people

Preconception: I will be the one who speaks to SLT about the issues that my team bring to me and I will solve them all! Power to the people!

The reality: Whilst you can challenge issues that impact your department and that you disagree with, you cannot solve every issue that your team members bring to you individually. Equally, some decisions are much higher than just at SLT level and no matter how much you badger SLT about something raised by a member of your team, they are much too busy to concern themselves with - what might be to them- something really quite trivial.

Solution: Listen to your team members, of course, but also encourage them to approach SLT with any personal issues that they are facing, to speak to their unions, and to raise relevant issues to HR if they deem necessary.

Teaching like the Boss I am

Preconception: My teaching is going to improve daily as a result of my all-seeing, middle-leader eye.

The reality: You are pulled in so many different directions as a middle leader that your teaching actually comes last, and that is okay because you are still able to deliver good lessons. However, the days of meticulously planning the placement of every dual-coded image on a PowerPoint slide are over.

Solution: Be satisfied that your teaching is good and stop trying to be the perfectionist in every single element of your role.

Luxuries

Preconception: I'll have my own office, which will have a Nespresso machine and cute little plants to make me feel really at home. Nobody will be able to steal my pastel highlighters!

The reality: You probably won't. Space is limited in schools. If you are fortunate enough to have an office (once known as a broom store) then don't fool yourself into thinking you'll need a Nespresso machine. The amount of time that you actually spend in that office alone is going to be minimal, and any time that you are in there doesn't mean you'll be sipping away on your macchiato at free will. You'll be meeting all the deadlines, replying to all the emails and being generally busy.

Solution: Be realistic. Your office is not a sanctuary in which to relax, it is a space to focus and get your job done; to Do Middle Leadership Right. Want a Nespresso machine in there? Fine. But don't expect to be able to subscribe on Amazon Prime for the pods, because you'll likely only use three in a term. You'll be the one rushing in and out of the staff room making an instant Nescafe before you know it. Like a new parent, you'll be drinking most of your hot drinks cold. Iced (tepid) latte, anyone?

I'm rich!

Preconception: With my new TLR it'll be holidays in Barbados every half term. I wonder how I commission a yacht….?

The reality: After tax, pension, and NI, your new TLR equates to an extra £57.32 per month.

Solution: Having more money is nice, especially when you've struggled through student life, paying off debts, buying first cars and houses, etc, but it's not the be-all and end-all, and it's probably not why we came into teaching (it was the holidays, right?). It's important to be remunerated for the job you are doing, and to feel valued and recognised, but we need to be realistic about school budgets too. That said, it's ok to talk to your peers about their salaries (there needs to be parity and clarity), and to ask for a pay rise or increment if you think you've earned it.

Top tips

- Manage your time carefully – write lists and be organised. It will make your life easier, and your team will appreciate your efficiency. Say no to things when you need to.

- Be kind to people – treat others as you would like to be treated. Make time for them. Show them you value them as people. Care. And be kind to yourself, too.

- Own up – we're all human and we all make mistakes or don't know things, and that's fine. Remember that fallibility is one positive quality found in good leaders; nobody is perfect so don't pretend to be. Ask for help and guidance when you need it.

- Don't expect celebrity treatment – respect is earnt and time is finite. Be present, be supportive and show an interest if you wish to be treated like the leader you've been appointed to be.

15 Conclusion

Congratulations on making it to the end of the book! But really, if you have read this far then you can rest assured that you have the right attitude for leadership, because you are seeking out knowledge to ensure you do a good job, and that shows that you care.

Caring is a huge part of leadership: caring for your team, your school, your students and yourself. And caring can mean making difficult, unpopular decisions; it can mean having difficult conversations; it can mean changing things and pushing people out of their comfort zones; it can mean saying no; it can mean challenging whole-school initiatives. And all of those can be hard to do. Leadership isn't easy, and sometimes middle leadership feels very difficult indeed.

Asking questions of yourself, being reflective of your practice, evaluating your leadership, are the marks of a good leader – one who isn't complacent or arrogant, one who doesn't think they have all the answers and one who is willing to learn.

We are privileged to work in schools, to serve our communities, to teach our students, and to support, empower and uplift our colleagues. But also, our schools, communities, colleagues and students are lucky to have us – remember that, and be proud of yourself for what you have achieved, and for the difference you make.

The highs and lows of middle leadership are worth it because of the positive impact you have on those around you, and the good you are doing. And by leading with your heart, and acting ethically, you are ***Doing Middle Leadership Right***.

DOI: 10.4324/9781003160557-16

Index